"For every woman who's ever believed something false, for every one of us who longs to be known and loved, Jerusha Clark's words and wisdom will lead you on the path to living more fully and beautifully. You will be left challenged and inspired to walk with Jesus in a whole new way."

Jill Savage, founder, Hearts at Home;
author, *No More Perfect Marriages*

"If you have ever doubted your worth, struggled with fear, or longed for a dynamic, satisfying faith, read this book! *Every Piece of Me* will help you to identity wrong thinking and lead you to a better understanding of who you really are as a follower of Jesus Christ. Jerusha Clark honestly shares her own toxic beliefs and vulnerably points her readers to transformed thinking based on a biblical belief system. I highly recommend this book for personal study and for small group use. An added bonus is an outstanding list of recommended books for going deeper on the subjects covered in each chapter. Don't miss this remarkable resource!"

Carol Kent, speaker; author, *Unquenchable: Grow a Wildfire Faith that Will Endure Anything*

"Jerusha's chapter on 'satisfying your true hunger' is *so* relevant—I can use this right away with the women we serve! Thank you, Jerusha, for sharing God's truth in such a practical way to bring freedom and balance to so many who need it."

Constance Rhodes, founder and CEO, FINDINGbalance, Inc.;
author, *Life Inside the "Thin" Cage*

"If you've ever wanted to have a wise counselor or big sister walking with you through the challenges of life, this book may be the answer. Jerusha writes like a friend who is beside you and who has been there, tackling the tough questions that plague every woman. There is true spiritual food and encouragement to be found in *Every Piece of Me*."

Dr. Juli Slattery, psychologist; co-founder, Authentic Intimacy

D1277732

"In *Every Piece of Me,* Jerusha invites us into a deeply honest, refreshing story that speaks to every woman in search of her true identity, worth, and purpose. This book reads like a dear friend, getting real next to me on the couch, curled up in a blanket, with a cup of hot tea or coffee, and a box of tissues between us. As a reader, I exhaled as I discovered that Jerusha's journey, like mine, has been rugged at times, and yet it has led her to the same place the Lord has led me: to look at God, the 'Great I AM,' for all that I am and all that I am meant to be. Thank you, Jerusha, for this poignant, beautiful book. It will no doubt help women everywhere discover the peace of knowing what they look like in God's heavenly eyes."

Jennifer Strickland, founder, URMore.org; speaker;
author, *21 Myths (Even Good) Girls Believe About Sex,
Beautiful Lies,* and *More Beautiful Than You Know*

Every Piece of Me

Shattering Toxic Beliefs and
DISCOVERING *the* REAL YOU

JERUSHA CLARK

BakerBooks

a division of Baker Publishing Group
Grand Rapids, Michigan

Published by Baker Books
a division of Baker Publishing Group
P.O. Box 6287, Grand Rapids, MI 49516-6287
www.bakerbooks.com

Printed in the United States of America

Library of Congress Cataloging-in-Publication Data is on file at the Library of Congress, Washington, DC.

ISBN 978-0-8010-0764-4

17 18 19 20 21 22 23   7 6 5 4 3 2 1

This book is dedicated
to my beloved Jeramy Alan,
for faithfully loving every piece of me
and
to my dear friends
Lynette Fuson and Rebekah Guzman,
who believed in these words when they were just impassioned ideas.

Contents

Introduction

I don't know what it is about church, but I'm always ravenous by the time the final worship song plays. In fact, if I'm not careful, my mind begins to wander to whatever delectable lunch options imagination presents. Have you experienced something similar?

Consider this: you're sitting in church, stomach starting to rumble while listening to the sermon, when suddenly the preacher proclaims, "I am the bread of life. If any of you are hungry, come, eat of me, and you will have life everlasting!"

Uhhh . . .

Or what if the next time you attended a memorial service, someone stood up and declared, "Don't be afraid! I am the resurrection and the life. If you believe in me, you will never die."

At our church, security would kindly—albeit firmly—escort someone who made these statements out the door. These are claims so dramatic that they border on the preposterous; on the lips of anyone I know, these words would sound insane.

Yet Jesus, the One on whom I stake my life and breath, made these very assertions. He also claimed to be the Light that expels all darkness, the True Vine, the Good Shepherd, the Door, and the Way.

These aren't exactly everyday declarations. Most people don't walk around comparing themselves to symbols of horticulture, animal care, or the natural world. But when Jesus makes these claims, they resonate with us in deep and undeniable ways. When Christ begins a phrase with "I am," his words reverberate grace and confidence in our hearts. He speaks truth that sets us free.

Why? How?

The story begins hundreds of years before Jesus's birth, when a man called Moses stumbled upon a bush that, though engulfed in flames, did not burn up. Unsurprisingly, this got Moses's attention. From within the fire, God declared, "I have indeed seen the misery of my people in Egypt. I have heard them crying out because of their slave drivers, and I am concerned about their suffering. So I have come down to rescue them. . . . [Moses,] I am sending you to Pharaoh to bring my people the Israelites out of Egypt," out of bondage, into the land of promise (see Exod. 3:2, 7–8, 10).

Moses was incredulous: *You want me to speak to the most powerful ruler in the world, God? On your behalf?! Why on earth would he listen to me?*

"Who should I say sent me?" Moses finally spluttered.

God responded simply: "Tell them *I AM* sent you" (see Exod. 3:11–14).

The Lord chooses to be known as Yahweh, the Great *I AM*. Throughout Scripture, he refers to himself more often by this name than any other. In doing so, God defines himself without reference to any thing, person, or trait. He *IS*, and that is enough.

Women find themselves in a far different situation. When we introduce ourselves, we typically describe ourselves in terms of our relationships (the wife, mother, daughter, sister, or friend of someone else) or in terms of our accomplishments (our title, position, education, or accolades). When our identity is wrapped up in these external things, however, we inevitably—and exhaustingly!—strive to prove ourselves worthy of love, attention, or affirmation.

God never meant for us to focus on whether we are "enough," whether we measure up. He made us—every piece of us—to *be* just as he *IS*.

I discovered this while exploring seven powerful statements made by Jesus and beginning with the same phrase—"I am." In using these words, Christ connects himself inextricably with the story of God's people and, more significantly, the revelation of God's very identity as the Great I AM. He shows himself to be the same yesterday, today, and forever (Heb. 13:8).

When Jesus came down, the unchangeable, eternal, all-powerful God opened himself to us. Through Christ, the Great I AM becomes personally knowable and lovable. He offers us the way, the truth, and life everlasting. Jesus invites us to fix our identity on God alone, freeing us from fear, bitterness, busyness, and other toxins that steal our joy and limit our influence for the kingdom. It's radical, earth shattering, and breathtakingly beautiful. I can't wait to explore it with you!

With kindness and wisdom, Jesus identifies himself with things we can understand, earthly things with which we have experience—bread, light, plants, doors. Christ's seven "I am" statements, recorded in John's Gospel, give us a glimpse into God's character and promises; they also highlight the contrasting opposites. Jesus is the answer not merely for our stomach pangs, but for our heartache as well; apart from him we experience hunger, exposure, and fruitlessness. Christ grants a way when we find ourselves lost, fullness when emptiness threatens, light when the darkness closes in. And he does not simply hand these things out as if they are quantities that can be depleted and will eventually run dry. By no means! Jesus *is* the Way, the Light, the Life we crave. Every piece of you was specifically and lovingly designed for his glory. He is—right now, in the present tense—everything: not just everything you need, but really, truly *everything*.

Humans often understand this poorly. I'm guilty as charged! Too many times I've taken "Jesus is everything" to mean Jesus will be "everything *I desire*." Christ does not claim "I am the antidepressant of life; I will make you feel better!" He does not promise "I am your district attorney; I'll get rid of those things or people that seem unjust." No one heard Jesus declare "I am the matchmaker" who will deliver you a happy marriage and family, nor "I am the financial planner who will satisfy your wildest dreams of security and success."[1]

His "I am" statements reveal that abundant life surpasses our limited vision. It goes beyond our comfort and is outside our control. Instead of sounding like good news to many of us, this sounds rather scary. Sadly, because many of us prefer safe, predictable, tidy lives, we sacrifice abundance to maintain the illusion of control.

Jesus's "I am" statements affirm that he *does* bring peace, justice, love, and freedom. He brings them on his perfect terms, however. More often than not, our qualms with the life of faith arise because our expectations of God neither match reality nor come to fruition. Understanding Jesus's "I am" statements helps us to *actually experience* the life of lavish abundance Christ died to give us. Enjoying this, however, requires total surrender, and most of us are slow to sign up for that.

According to 1 Timothy 6:15, Jesus is the blessed controller of all things. He *must* be in control of your life and mine because— brace yourself, here—you and I have no power whatsoever to save ourselves. Why? Because we need to be saved from the one thing we can never escape. A good deal of the time, I can get away from situations, locations, and relationships, but I can never escape myself. Neither can you, my friend. We cannot outrun what we've done, what we deserve, who we are. Our only hope is in a God who draws near, a God who comes down, a God who is not only in control but *good* at controlling everything.

This is—praise be to God!—precisely who Jesus is. He is the God who enters our world and refuses to leave. He refuses to leave us alone, refuses to leave us in our sin, refuses to leave even when we push him away. Jesus's "I am" statements radically transform who

I am; in each of these seven claims, Jesus reveals core truths about his character, our heavenly Father's character, and the character of the Spirit who dwells in us. You and I cannot remain the same after encountering the Great I AM.

I am so excited to delve into each of Jesus's "I am" statements with you. In order to do that, we'll look first at the Great I AM before Jesus came to earth. The study of God's chosen name has been life-changing for me. I pray and believe it will be the same for you (even if your stomach rumbles while you read).

{1}

Since You Are Precious and Honored . . .

Some years ago, I developed a guiding principle, a single sentence that expresses my commitment to live in spring or winter, in times of plenty or times of want. With the eager anticipation that it may alter the course of your life, as it has done mine, I have determined to share this profound philosophy with you: Life is too short to wear ugly socks.

Why settle for the mundane when you can enjoy footwear exploding with color and pattern, socks for every holiday, socks that make life just a little more fun?

I collect funky socks. It's a cheap way to add flavor to my life, and though it's not as weighty a philosophical statement as I pretended it to be, I truly am a sock lover.

While I'm admitting odd things about myself, I'll just go ahead and inform you that I'm also an adrenaline junkie. To scratch my itch for a natural high, I've taken a trapeze class (amazing), zip-lined upside down in the Mexican rain forest (equally phenomenal), and tackled some of the world's most ferocious roller coasters (bring it on, baby).

I am also a pastor's wife, the mother of two teenage girls (you now know how to pray for me), and the daughter of a film and television composer.

Is this the sum total of who I am: a wife, a mommy, a sock collector, a thrill-seeker, a girl who grew up in the shadow of Hollywood? Over the course of my life, I've certainly defined myself in these ways . . . or others. I've also wrestled with a desire to be identified with something more interesting, someone more important—or at least less of a mess—than myself, something grander and greater than just little old me.

Perhaps you've longed, as I have, for meaning, purpose, and a sense of self that *transcends*. I suspect you have, even if years of unfulfilled dreams, hopes, and expectations have buried that yearning or turned it bitter in your memory. Humans—and women in particular—ache to be part of something beautiful, important, and enduring.

While preparing to teach a women's retreat several years ago, I stumbled across an idea that radically altered my understanding of identity and purpose. At the time, I was struggling with how to open the first session; getting a retreat off on the right foot is important to speaker and attendees alike, so I was eager to figure something out (preferably something brilliant). In moments like these, I sometimes turn back to my favorite passages of Scripture, both because being reminded of God's truth centers me and also because I find that he teaches me new things with every rereading. This occasion was no exception. As my eyes fell on Isaiah 43, these words reverberated in my heart and mind:

> But now, this is what the Lord says—
>   he who created you, Jacob,
>   he who formed you, Israel:
> "Do not fear, for I have redeemed you;
>   I have summoned you by name; you are mine.

When you pass through the waters,
    I will be with you;
and when you pass through the rivers,
    they will not sweep over you.
When you walk through the fire,
    you will not be burned;
    the flames will not set you ablaze.
For *I am* the Lord your God,
    the Holy One of Israel, your Savior; . . .
you are precious and honored in my sight,
    and because I love you,
I will give people in exchange for you,
    nations in exchange for your life. . . .
You are my witnesses," declares the Lord,
    "and my servant whom I have chosen,
so that you may know and believe me
    and understand that I am he. . . .
I, even *I, am* the Lord,
    and apart from me there is no savior.
I have revealed and saved and proclaimed—
    I, and not some foreign god among you.
You are my witnesses," declares the Lord, "that I am
    God.
    Yes, and from ancient days *I am* he." (vv. 1–4, 10–13,
    emphasis added)

With these proclamations, God reiterates his name, the name he revealed to Moses through fire, the name he used to seal his covenant with a people chosen to be his treasured possession, the name that speaks unparalleled power, perfect presence, and all-surpassing wisdom:

I AM.

God eternal, God exalted, God with reference to no other thing or person, activity or achievement. God alone, the Great I AM.

Marveling at God's greatness, it also struck me forcefully: God, the Great I AM, tells me who I am.

Living Out Your True Identity

Thrilled by what God was stirring in my mind, I dove into a Hebrew word study of Isaiah 43. I could barely contain my excitement as I prepared to teach women what the Great I AM says about who they are—chosen, free, secure, precious, honored, and beloved. These were neither words I came up with to bolster spirits exhausted by the cares and endless obligations of life, nor ideas I conjured to pump up deflated self-esteems; these were the very words God chose, with deliberate and loving intention, to define who I am. They determine who you are too.

I am purposefully formed; so implies Isaiah 43, verses 1 and 7. The adverb "purposefully" connotes not merely the express intention, but also the significance and meaning of whatever it describes. You and I have been formed on purpose and for a purpose. You've likely heard that before, and perhaps you believe it. Or maybe you assent to it intellectually, but don't actually live as if it's true. Let's look closer at what the Word of God teaches.

Isaiah uses three distinct Hebrew words to illuminate the purposefulness of your identity. I am—and you are—created (*bara'*), formed (*yatsar*), and made (*'asah*). *Bara'*, in some ways the simplest of these terms, means "brought into being." *Yatsar* points to a creation determined ahead of time, then molded or squeezed into shape. And *'asah* indicates something prepared and put in order for a purpose. Taking these rich Hebrew words together, we discover that God deliberately formed each of our individual identities by bringing us into being, molding us into a unique shape, and specifically preparing us to do and be good (later confirmed by the Lord's words in Ephesians 2:10).

In Isaiah 43:1 and 7, the Great I AM also tells me that I am chosen. You must think beyond just "selected" here; this is no schoolyard pick in which you might be the last one, waiting to hear a deep sigh and, "I guess I'll take . . ." No! This word for "chosen," *bachar*, connotes preference and longing. You aren't simply selected by God to fill up his team. *He yearns for you and is partial to you.* Isn't that wonderful?!

According to Isaiah 43:4, you are also precious, honored, and beloved. The Hebrew word for love used in this context, *'ahab,* means "passionately cherished and desired"; it's a provocative term, a word that indicates a profound and lasting love that is not contingent on deserving, but rather freely given, highly prized, and mutually rewarding. Being precious—*yaqar*—in his eyes means that you are valuable to him, a costly treasure he wants and delights in.

This is not my way of trying to make you feel good about yourself. This is your God, the Great I AM speaking. He calls you beloved, precious, and honored. The Hebrew term *kabed,* translated as "honored," means "held in high regard and treated with respect." Whatever your past, whether you've been esteemed or abused by other people, your Creator thinks highly of you. Indeed, this same word—*kabed*—is associated with the Hebrew term for God's glory, the weightiness of his splendor and majesty. The Great I AM says that I am his highly prized, glorious beloved. You, too, are precious; you are honored; you are loved.

Do you believe it? Does what you believe change the way you live day by day?

Perhaps this all seems trite to you, or too good to be true. Maybe you can accept it on a cognitive level, but your heart is weighed down by messages you've heard and sensed for as long as you can remember: not good enough, too much *this* and too little *that,* broken, needy, worthless. Maybe you've felt trapped by these lies or others.

I have lived in similar bondage. I've also been told repeatedly by family and friends that I am loved. Despite the fact that I've been blessed with these affirmations, all too often encouraging words have failed to penetrate the depth of who I am.

Here's why. If I don't believe that the Great I AM tells me who I am, and if you don't determine to live in that truth, too, no amount of "learning to love yourself," no set of accomplishments or achievements, no measure of human affection will fill the gaping hole inside, the place where identity is formed. You and I can choose to remain trapped in our own "I am . . ." thoughts, or we can be set free by the Great I AM.

Isaiah 43 proclaims that you and I have been redeemed, *ga'al*, bought back from slavery. When sin entered the world, your identity and mine were shattered along with everything else. We became slaves to iniquity, claims the apostle Paul in Romans 6. According to the Great I AM's words in Isaiah 43, we are set free—*ga'al*—from this bondage, both to the sin we choose and the sin perpetrated against us. Whether you have consciously believed lies about your identity or subtly absorbed them from the culture and people surrounding you, you can be set free. Indeed, you have already been set free. The prison door has been unlocked, the ransom for your life paid by Jesus. Your part is to let the shackles fall and walk out, embracing your freedom step-by-step.

To redeem and restore us, to set us free, the Great I AM paid a high price for us. The Hebrew word used in Isaiah 43 for "exchange," or "ransom"—*kopher*—is a particularly fascinating one. It connotes both the cost of a life and also a covering (the example given in my Hebrew-English parallel Bible is pitch, the thick, tarlike substance that seals a roof). The Great I AM truly has "got you covered" (*kopher*), protected and secure.

I had begun to study this passage in order to teach others, but I became personally captivated by it, transformed with every new discovery. My excitement to teach the retreat grew exponentially. The Great I AM tells me who I am! I couldn't wait to share the truth: every piece of us is marked by his intentional purpose, his calling on our lives!

Isaiah 43 uses the word "call," *qara'*, three different times, beginning in verse one: "I have called you by name; you are Mine" (NASB). I absolutely love this word, *qara'*. It means "to summon, invite, commission, and endow." The Great I AM has called you into—appointed you to and empowered you for—a life of purpose, freedom, belovedness, and honor. Breathtaking!

Here's what really gets me about *qara'*, though. The word indicates crying out loudly. It literally carries the meanings "to accost" and to "confront boldly." God cares enough about me to get my attention, whatever it takes. When the Great I AM tells me who I am, it matters to him that I hear it. It matters to him that you are listening to his call too. Are you?

When we discuss the "call" of God, we often speak of his plan for our time, our work and service, the way we should spend our days here on earth. While this is certainly part of his call on our lives, we cannot limit his *qara'* to that. You see, *qara'* also means "to give name to," and this is what pulls all of the intricacies of Isaiah 43 together. The Great I AM has given you a name: Beloved. He has called you by name: Precious. He died to secure your name: Honored, covered, called as his own. Now you get to choose. *Will I live into who he says I am?*

Psychologists define *cognitive dissonance* as the mental stress, often accompanied by physical symptoms of tension, experienced by those who hold—consciously or subconsciously—two or more contradictory beliefs, ideas, or values at the same time. Because humans naturally seek to make sense of their existence and are incessant interpreters of the world around and inside them, living in *cognitive dissonance* produces both internal chaos and external strain.[1]

Tragically, many of us plod through our days in spiritual dissonance, "knowing" a lot about God yet experiencing little of the love, mercy, and grace we claim to believe he provides. Indeed, "the lives of many Christians are an argument in which their heads tell them one thing while their hearts assert the opposite. . . . [They] understand the doctrine of God's love, but [they] may not know how to receive and experience this love, secretly wondering if God even likes them."[2] This dissonance creates a divide, not only internally, between head and heart, but also relationally, between the God of truth and his beloved, precious, and highly honored daughters.

Because we are confronted—each and every day—with evidence that we don't deserve to be loved, that we don't have our act together and won't anytime soon, that we're actually far more broken and needy and sinful in the secret places of our minds and hearts than we'd dare admit and would rather not consider, we battle the tension of "knowing" God's truth and "knowing" the reality of our condition at the same time. Is there hope for this sad predicament?

By the grace of God, yes! But it won't come by doing our best to prove that we're not as bad as we think we are (and may, in plain fact, actually be). Rather, it will come by allowing the Great I AM to breathe his truth into every piece of us, down to the very core of our identity. If I truly believe that I am who he says I am, *everything* changes. The same is true for you.

We simply cannot move forward without that knowledge. Indeed, I'm firmly convinced that it is impossible for us to face the wounds of our past and the sins we avoid thinking about without an experiential understanding of God's love. Without the truth of your belovedness, preciousness, and esteem in God's eyes girding you up, the burdens of life are insupportable. When we lack awareness and conviction of God's unconditional love, we turn to lesser loves: control, order, the affections of people, acquisitions, and achievements.

You may have excellent theology when it comes to God's love and your identity. You may believe all the "right things," but "*good theology only helps when it controls the inner life. . . .* Biblical doctrine is often used as a protective shield to keep the inner life away from God's control."[3] If we claim to believe truth, yet hide the depths of our identity from the God who formed us, redeemed us, and calls us by name, we remain trapped in something far worse than psychological dissonance; we sell our birthright as the beloved for the bondage of self-preservation.

We witness the implications of this beginning in Isaiah 43:8, where a startling transition occurs. From words laced with love and intimacy (vv. 1–7), God shifts to a bold and—at least in my thinking—curious command: "Lead out those who have eyes but are blind, who have ears but are deaf" (v. 8). In the verses that follow, the biblical scene shifts to an allegorical courtroom, and a symbolic legal battle ensues. The prosecution: God, the Great I AM. On the defensive: the false gods of each nation surrounding Israel, God's treasured possession. The matter at stake: Who controls the earth, human history, and those within it?

What does this have to do with God's identity and ours? How does this connect with the profound words the Great I AM uses to tell me who I am?

The first clue comes as God calls for evidence to be presented in this allegorical case. Yahweh demands that the nations bring proof of their gods' actions, confirmation of what the gods they've worshiped—and seduced God's people into worshiping—have done. There is, of course, not one corroborating testimony, not one shred of evidence for the world's idols.

In what I consider a shocking (and a bit risky) move, God the Prosecutor launches his offensive by declaring to his people: "'*You* are my witnesses . . . and my servant whom I have chosen, so that you may know and believe me and understand that *I am*. . . . Before me no god was formed, nor will there be one after me. I, even *I*, *am* the Lord, and apart from me there is no savior. I have revealed and saved and proclaimed—I, and not some foreign god among you. You are my witnesses,' declares the Lord, 'that *I am*'" (Isa. 43:10–12, italics mine).

The word "witness" used in Isaiah 43 is *ayd*, literally "evidence" or "testimony." This term is incredibly significant for your identity and mine. Not only am I his precious, beloved, and honored one, I am also the proof of who he is. The Great I AM tells me who I am and—in a beautiful chiasmus—who I am should reveal the Great I AM. I am his witness and you are too.

This means that living out your true identity is far more than a personal concern; it matters to the whole world that I am an authentic reflection of the Great I AM. If you and I fail to provide evidence of our belovedness, God's truth remains hidden from a world full of those who desperately need it. Discovering who I am is not a luxury that I can explore when I have the time (after the kids are grown?) or if I have the temperament (some people are just more "into" that sort of thing than others, right?). By no means! Who I am *must* reveal the Great I AM. The same is true for you. And this truth *must* alter our daily lives—our dealing with the insurance company, grocery shopping, earning a wage, all the while wishing we had a little more time, day-to-day lives. Who I am should point a broken world to God as the Great I AM.

This is what I want; it's what I'm *made for*! But I'll be honest with you: even though the Great I AM tells me who I am, I often live as if who I am depends on those around me, what I do (or fail to do), or what I have. That's why being connected with someone who seems cooler (my Hollywood dad), more "together" or more important than me (my pastor husband and you'll-be-well-rounded-if-I-die-making-it-happen kids) still pulls at my heart. Whereas I identify myself in these ways—"I'm Jeramy's wife," "I'm Jocelyn and Jasmine's mom," "I'm a writer"—God refers to himself with relation to no one and nothing but himself: I AM who I AM, He declares (Exod. 3:14).

Jesus wants us to follow this example and stake our identity on what he says about us and *that alone*. Okay, I'm a sock collector and a thrill-seeker, a mommy and a wife, but those things just describe me. They don't *define* me. Here's who I really am: Purposefully formed. Called. Chosen. Ransomed and redeemed. Precious. Honored. Beloved.

You are, too—undeniably. Irrevocably. Every piece of you, without exception.

In the next chapter, we'll look at what keeps us from living out this truth, the truth of our identity. Breaking free from false identities requires serious remodeling of our thoughts, decisions, and desires. That ain't easy, but as Jesus removes the obstacles that threaten to overwhelm us, we recapture the joy of our identity. Shattering toxic beliefs and choosing truth enables you to discover the *real you*. And that, my friend, is worth fighting for.

~~~~

Questions for Personal Reflection or Group Discussion

1. Is it easy or difficult for you to believe that you are precious, honored, and beloved? Why?

2. Does your daily life reflect what you claim to believe? If someone observed you for one month, could they confidently affirm that you see yourself as secure, free, called, and chosen?

3. What do you imagine are some of the "obstacles" mentioned at the end of this chapter, the things that threaten to steal the joy of your true identity?

Recommended Reading

- Chapian, Mary. *His Thoughts Toward Me: Daily Meditations for Friends of God.* Minneapolis: Bethany House, 1987.
- Nouwen, Henri. *Life of the Beloved: Spiritual Living in a Secular World.* New York: Crossroad Publishing Company, 2002.

{2}

Do You Want To Be Well?

I'll take a wild stab in the dark here: you probably don't bow down to a bird statue in your spare time. I feel pretty safe in assuming that you don't have a gilded image of a sea creature on a dais in your home. Neither do I. I do, however, have a serious problem with misplaced worship.

The Bible has a word for this. It's a word all too often dismissed as archaic or "Old Testament." The word is *idolatry*, and it's just as significant an issue for you and me today as it was for the ancient Israelites, to whom God gave the command, "You shall have no other gods before me. You shall not make for yourself an image in the form of anything in heaven above or on the earth beneath or in the waters below. You shall not bow down to them or worship them" (Exod. 20:3–5a). I've never offered a sacrifice to a golden calf, but misplaced worship is still the biggest and most dangerous obstacle to living my true identity as Christ's precious, honored, and beloved daughter.

Idols perpetually clamor for the affection of my heart and yours. Each and every decision is part of a war of worship fought on the battlefield of your mind and heart. Our twenty-first-century idols—e.g., family, love, success, security, control—may take form and shape in *seemingly* safer and less idolatrous ways than graven images of old, but they enslave our hearts nonetheless. My idols make me less than who I am, who I *truly* am, and your idols are bent on systematically destroying you as well. Worship is never neutral. It sustains life or consumes it. Worship surrenders glory or seeks to steal it. And what we worship—what we love and order our lives around—inevitably defines who we are.

In Isaiah 43, God specifically links the breathtaking proclamation of his presence with us through the fires and floods of life, our preciousness and honor in his eyes, and our role as his witnesses with the issue of worship (see vv. 9–13). He does this because worship is far more about identity than it is about activity. We participate in worshipful activities because we *are* worshipers at the core of our being. Your identity as the beloved is inextricably tied to your identity as one who worships. Who I am depends upon what I worship as fully as my body depends upon the beat of my heart and the breath of my lungs (Ps. 135:15, 18). You and I are together in this; our identity and our worship are inseparable.

It's radical to consider, however: though worship is sewn into our identity, we are not *compelled* to worship any one thing. God is the ultimate gentleman in this regard. He invites and woos, but does not force. I choose the object of my worship and you choose too. But choose wisely, for we become like the things, people, or achievements in which we place our trust.

For many years, I assumed that an idol had to be something "bad." I didn't worship money; that was clearly *wrong.* But I did pay homage to the yearning in my heart for security. I wouldn't worship sex like some of those "ancient barbarians," but as a single woman I arranged much of my life around the quest for love and romance with little concern for the safety of my heart. I would never dream of worshiping food like the cultures Paul confronts in his epistle to the Philippians, but I saw no problem in perpetuating the enmity between my soul and my body, trying to control its aging, aching, or appearance with diet, exercise, and the terribly ineffective but ever-present draw of worry. Trouble is, when you believe that an idol has to be something *evidently evil*, you miss the idols that creep in through the back door of your heart and mind.

Timothy Keller's powerful and convicting book *Counterfeit Gods* helped me see that the most insidious idols are good things that I simply, and mistakenly, try to make ultimate things.[1] Kyle Idleman's *Gods at War* also helped transform my thinking. Indeed, claims Idleman, "The more beautiful a thing is, the more capacity it has to become an idol. The more I fear losing it, the more likely I am to worship it."[2] Perhaps you're ahead of me in this game; maybe none of this comes as a surprise to you, as it did to me when I first began studying it. Whatever the level of your knowledge, however, I am confident that idolatry is still an issue for you, as it is for me. Why? Because every sin points to misplaced worship, and we all wrestle with sin.

Every outburst of anger reveals misdirected worship (for me it's usually because an idol of comfort or control has been threatened and exposed). Every little deception—for example, saying "I *can't* do it that night" when really you just don't want to attend that event or take care of your friends' kids—uncovers an idol of the heart. (Relational idols are some of the most subtly destructive.) According to God, our idols may not be immediately obvious, but they are constantly warring for our attention and affection. In Ezekiel 14, he reveals that people "set up idols *in their hearts*" (v. 3, emphasis added).

If none of us deliberately desires to be an idolater, how do idols take control of us? Tim Keller shrewdly observes, "There are 'deep idols' within the heart, beneath the more concrete and visible 'surface idols' that we serve. Sin in our hearts affects our basic motivational drives so they become idolatrous, 'deep idols.'" Surface idols are things such as money, career, our spouse or children, things "through which our deep idols seek fulfillment." In other words, surface idols dictate our behavior, but deep idols shape the fabric of who we are more powerfully. Deep idols become obstacles to living as our true and best selves because they are woven into our thoughts and motives, the place where identity is formed.[3]

Because of this, misplaced worship manifests uniquely in each individual. "Some people," for instance,

> are strongly motivated by a desire for influence and power, while others are more excited by approval and appreciation. Some want emotional and physical comfort more than anything else, while still others want security [or] the control of their environment. . . . For example, money can be a surface idol that serves to satisfy more foundational impulses. Some people want lots of money as a way to control their world and life. Such people usually don't spend much money and live very modestly. They keep it all safely saved and invested, so they can feel completely secure in the world. Others want money for access to social circles and to make themselves beautiful and attractive. These people *do* spend their money on themselves in lavish ways. Other people want money because it gives them so much power over others. In every case, money functions as an idol and yet, because of various deep idols, it results in very different patterns of behavior. Each deep idol—power, approval, comfort, or control—generates a different set of fears and a different set of hopes.[4]

For this reason, we cannot deal only with our idolatrous behavior; that leads to a superficial analysis and an attack on the strongholds our idols will viciously defend. In order to defeat the idols clamoring for our worship, the idols that keep us from the truth of our identity as God's beloved, chosen witnesses, we must wade into the complex regions of the heart and mind, the lair of deep idols.

Take a moment and consider a few surface idols: family, career and education (yours or your kids'), entertainment, and physical pleasure (perhaps mediated through food, fitness, or affection). Think about the ways these concrete things are tied to motivations that rule our hearts on the deepest levels: longings

for comfort or security, the yearning for freedom and opportunity, our lust for control—even if only over our own lives or
our spouses and children—and our ache for approval. Can you
begin to see the way these cries of the heart take form and shape
in idol worship?

Your identity, and the life you live out of it, is determined by
what you worship. And what we worship is determined both pas-
sively, by what we're exposed to, and actively, by what we *choose*
to think about. As our minds absorb what surrounds us, as we
focus our attention on certain things and not others, our lives take
shape. That which we worship becomes resident in our hearts and
minds, and our thoughts then motivate actions and words. Everything glorious and everything hideous begins with a thought. In
this way, what you choose to worship becomes "the one choice
that all other choices are motivated by."[5]

Because of this, and in a somewhat odd turn of events, you can't
experience God's love without confronting the deep sin of your
own heart. My idols are obstacles to living out my true identity;
the same is true for you. Pretending idolatry doesn't affect us leads
only to spiritual dissonance and separation from the Great I AM.
In tender mercy, he leads us to a crossroads and invites you and
me to choose . . . *This day*, whom will you serve?

God asked his military commander and committed servant,
Joshua, the same question thousands of years ago. He asks each of
us this too. How will you respond? "But if serving the Lord seems
undesirable to you," Joshua told the Israelites, "then choose for
yourselves this day whom you will serve, whether the gods your
ancestors served beyond the Euphrates, or the gods of the Amorites,
in whose land you are living. But as for me and my household, we
will serve the Lord" (Josh. 24:15).

Choose. *This day.*

If you genuinely want to serve the Lord and live out your true
identity, I encourage you to ponder the following idol-revealing
questions:[6]

- What do you daydream about? Where do your thoughts naturally go when you're alone, say, sitting at a stoplight or sipping your coffee?
- What do you complain about most?
- What worries you most?
- What disappoints you most?
- For what do you make financial sacrifices?
- Where do you go when you're hurting? Do you head for the fridge? Call a friend? Flip on the TV or click on the computer?

The everyday things that occupy our energies, that consume our thoughts and determine what we lament, get frustrated by, feel wounded because of, and hope for reveal the deep idols of our hearts, the worship that moves us to act and speak. It's not easy to answer these questions truthfully. Sadly, most of us would rather live with the tension of spiritual dissonance than allow God to tackle the idols of our hearts. Surrendering an idol of control or comfort to Jesus can initially feel excruciatingly painful, along the lines of what happened once upon a time to a self-centered boy who turned into a dragon after lying too long on hoarded treasure, "with greedy, dragonish thoughts in his heart."

Such was the case in C. S. Lewis's classic tale, *The Voyage of the Dawn Treader*. Lewis's character, Eustace Scrubb, confesses to his friends that it was a more harrowing experience not to *become* a dragon but to *stop* being one:

> I was lying awake and wondering what on earth would become of me [when] I looked up and saw the very last thing I expected: a huge lion coming slowly toward me. . . . I shut my eyes tight. But that wasn't any good because it told me to follow it. . . .
>
> Then the lion said . . . "You will have to let me undress you."
>
> I was afraid of his claws, . . . but I was pretty nearly desperate now. So I just lay flat down on my back to let him do it.

The very first tear he made was so deep that I thought it had gone right into my heart. And when he began pulling the [dragon] skin off, it hurt worse than anything I've ever felt. The only thing that made me able to bear it was just the pleasure of feeling the stuff peel off. . . .

And there was I smooth and soft as a peeled switch and smaller than I had been. Then he caught hold of me—I didn't like that much for I was very tender underneath now that I'd no skin on—and threw me into the water. It smarted like anything but only for a moment. After that . . . I found that all the pain had gone. . . . And then I saw why. I'd turned into a boy again.[7]

In his mercy, Aslan (Lewis's Christ figure) rips the dragon scales from Eustace's body, freeing him from reptilian imprisonment. The agony was tremendous, but it was also momentary. Restoration made him "tender" and "smaller" at first, but ultimately whole and healed, his true and best self.

Before Aslan first appears to Eustace and tells him the dragon hide must come off, the boy has attempted—and failed—three times to rend the scales from his own body. Every time, despite Eustace's desire to be free and regardless of the fervor with which he tears at himself, the hard, rough, wrinkled, and scaly skin returns. Only Aslan can liberate Eustace from the dragon hide, the result of his bondage to dragonish thoughts in his dragonish heart.

I hate that I, too, have ugly thoughts. I want comfort more than joy in trials and perseverance. I long for control, not wholehearted surrender. I want love without having to face the darkness of my heart. I am not given that option. But I *am* given a choice, and so are you. Will we let the Great I AM rend the idols that cling to us like dragon hide? Will we allow him not only to remove them but also replace them?

My friend, it will not do to simply root out your idols. The temptation, when faced with the depth of our misplaced worship, is to become idol hunters, captivated with a quest: I will destroy my idols, whatever the cost! This sounds well and good, but the truth is, rejecting a false god does not mean you have embraced the True and Living One. To live into your true identity, you must be captivated by what Scottish theologian Thomas Chalmers called "the expulsive power of a new affection."

In his sermon after the same name, Chalmers warned those who focused inordinately on exposing idols, while failing to redirect worship to God: It is not enough that we eloquently speak against the idol, nor even that we expose its illusiveness. No, we must allow ourselves to be transfixed by something else, something strong enough to transfer the affection of our heart and mind to a greater, truer, more enduring hope.[8]

In other words, you and I must become captivated by the power of an affection for God so complete and true that it not only expels idols, but supplants them. That's my hope for this book. I pray that, in meeting Jesus as the Great I AM, both the confused *and* the sinful impulses within us will be—all at once—torn away and replaced with redeemed thoughts and renewed hearts. God has promised to do this for all who will allow it: "I will give you a new heart, and I will put a new spirit in you. I will take out your stony, stubborn heart and give you a tender, responsive heart" (Ezekiel 36:26 NLT).

The question remains: *Do you really want it?*

When Jesus walked this earth, he often surprised people with his curiosity. Reread the Gospels; our Lord appears downright inquisitive! Perhaps you recall the story of a man who spent thirty-eight years waiting to be healed, only to be shoved out of the way time and time again by the more assertive, the more successful, the "lucky ones" who had help. Jesus comes along and asks him: "Do you want to get well?" (John 5:6).

Nearly four decades this man had been waiting. Thirty-eight years of adjusting and compensating and shaming and yearning. How could he *not* want to be well? And yet . . .

The man doesn't respond, "Absolutely!" Instead, he recites the list of reasons healing has eluded him. Were our situations reversed, were I thirty-eight years in the grip of a horrible affliction and asked, "Do you want to be healed?" I hope that I would just say *yes*!

But wait; this is precisely where I find myself: in the throes of a great battle with an ancient enemy, suffering from a disease of misplaced worship that cripples not my legs, but my mind and heart, my relationships and expectations. Do I want to get well? Do you want to get well?

The Well That Never Runs Dry

Because I believe you, like I, long not only to be free but also to truly live in that freedom each and every day, I invite you to journey with me. As we look at the life-changing "I am" statements of Jesus, we'll discover that the Great I AM redeems and restores us by revealing who he is. As who he is becomes who I am, and as it does for you as well, the truth of our belovedness, our preciousness, and our eternal esteem in his eyes sinks down into the marrow of our bones and the automatic thoughts of our hearts. In this way, even if no unfavorable circumstance of our lives changes, even when trials come (and we know they will), *even then* everything will be different, for we will be different.

The Bible has a word for this too. In Greek, it's *metanoia*, a change of mind. Our modern translations render the word as "repentance." It's a new way of seeing and thinking, an eradication of old, faulty thoughts and a vigilant commitment to build and guard new ones. It is the substance of our faith, this *metanoia*. Any true change in how we live starts with faith, with repentance, with a progressive and wholesale reordering of the mind and heart that transforms every word and deed.

That's why, in this book, we'll focus heavily on the thoughts you are thinking and the habits you've established. What you choose to love and what you daily do because of that love changes you from the inside out. What you and I think about God, what I think about who I am, what you believe about who you are matters *a great deal*. I appreciate the straightforward way Proverbs 4:23 is sometimes translated: "Be careful what you think, because your thoughts run your life" (NCV).

I first memorized that verse in the New International Version: "Above all else, guard your heart, for everything you do flows from it." When you understand that the biblical Hebrew word for "heart" encompasses the will, emotions, and mind, it's easy to see why Proverbs 4:23 commands, in essence, *Watch out! Your life is determined by what you think about.*

The entire focus of my adult ministry has been helping women evaluate their thought lives and allow God to redeem them. This book is no exception. And yet, we must *practice* the substance of our repentance to truly get well and worship rightly; we must develop new habits based on God's love for us and ours for him. "Faith without works" isn't just weak, it's flat-out dead (James 2:17).

For this reason, each chapter will also provide what I hope will be practical opportunities for you to say, and live out, a *yes* to Christ's query: *Do you want to get well?* From this point on, every chapter will close with an invitation to try a spiritual practice. Some of them are ancient spiritual disciplines that centuries of Christians have enjoyed. Some you will take to like the proverbial duck to water; others may strike you as odd or uncomfortable. That's okay. No spiritual practice is meant to be prescriptive; they are merely tools to prepare our hearts and place us before the God who heals, the God who whispers his truth to us as he calls us by name.

As this chapter comes to a close, I invite you to practice what you might call "the prayer of belovedness." As you do so, remember that this is no formula, but rather a guide to direct your thoughts in the presence of God.

Here's how it works. Spend some time locating three (or more) verses that speak of God's love for you. It's not cheating to use Isaiah 43! I also love Jeremiah 31:3 and Isaiah 54:10, though I highly encourage you to discover your own as well. If you're new to a process like this, using a concordance or an online Bible search tool to look up "God's love" can be a tremendous help.

Now slowly read the verses you've selected. Reread them out loud, placing your name in the verse. We can practice this right now using the first seven verses of Isaiah 43: "*This is what the Lord says—he who created you, _____, he who formed you. 'Do not fear, for I have redeemed you; _____, I have summoned you by name; you are mine. When you pass through the waters, I will be with you; and when you pass through the rivers, they will not sweep over you. When you walk through the fire, you will not be burned; the flames will not set you ablaze. For I am the Lord your God, the Holy One of Israel, your Savior. . . . _____, you are precious and honored in my sight, and because I love you, I will give people in exchange for you, nations in exchange for your life.*" Listen to the words as you read them. You can say something in response such as, "Thank you, Lord, for speaking this to me and about me. I claim this to be true because you *are* true."

You have just prayed the prayer of belovedness. By receiving his Word into your mind and heart, by responding with thankfulness and affirming his truth, you have worshiped the Great I AM. Your feelings about yourself may not have changed with immediacy; we should not expect to unravel, in a matter of moments, thoughts that have taken decades to form (particularly if they are pernicious, negative ones). God is certainly able to do this; his Word *is* that powerful, sharper than a two-edged sword. He is also, however, the God of slow growth, the God of the journey as much as the destination. He is producing spiritual fruit in you that may—indeed, likely will—take time to ripen. I encourage you to practice the prayer of belovedness often, to make it a habit. His truth can become to you like a fount of living water, refreshing your soul. His well never runs dry.

In Jeremiah 2:13, the Lord laments that his people "have forsaken me, the spring of living water, and have dug their own cisterns, broken cisterns that cannot hold water." In other words, they've fashioned worthless, leaking cistern-idols, while he wants to quench their thirst eternally. God's merciful solution: to send Jesus, the Great I AM in human flesh, to proclaim, "Whoever drinks the water I give them will never thirst. Indeed, the water I give them will become in them a spring of water welling up to eternal life" (John 4:14).

If you're done with trying to drink from a broken cup, I invite you to taste and see that living in your true identity—as the Lord's beloved, precious, chosen, and honored one—is good. *Very good.*

~~~~~

Questions for Personal Reflection or Group Discussion

1. Choose one of the "idol-revealing" questions on page 32 and journal about or discuss your response.
2. How would you describe the difference between the following approaches to misdirected worship: being an "idol hunter" and being captivated by the power of a greater affection for God?
3. Explore the question "Do you want to get well?" In what ways might this apply to your life right now?

Recommended Reading

- Idleman, Kyle. *Gods at War: Defeating the Idols that Battle for Your Heart.* Grand Rapids: Zondervan, 2013.
- Keller, Tim. *Counterfeit Gods: The Empty Promises of Money, Sex, and Power, and the Only Hope That Matters.* New York: Dutton, 2009.

{3}

From Fear To Freedom

In my early twenties, I became friends with Gigi, a woman in her late seventies. Gigi and I were pen pals (yes, these do exist!), exchanging long letters on topics as varied as curry recipes, dog training, and eternal life. Somehow it all made sense over the course of our correspondence.

A fascinating and creative woman, Gigi had survived the Great Depression, served as a nurse during World War II, taught herself woodcarving, and played the organ in her spare time. Smart as a whip, sharp-tongued on occasion, yet tenderhearted at the core, Gigi and I condensed life into tiny script, scrawled on cards, sealed and stamped and mailed with love.

Though we shared so much, Gigi often described her faith in terms that troubled me. While we both believed in God and agreed on a general biblical narrative, Gigi—particularly as she grew older and frailer—wrote with anxiety about her eternal state. "I just hope I've done enough . . . ," she expressed. It seemed eternal life was primarily about *relief* for her: no more striving to prove herself, no more wondering whether she was good enough. A settled spiritual unrest, like a dull pain or a noise that's been there so long you almost forget when it first started, marked her letters. I'm positive it was engraved on her heart too.

I attended Gigi's funeral shortly before my thirtieth birthday. Here I was, on the verge of a new chapter in life, full of vim and vigor, standing at the graveside of a woman I deeply loved, a bright and unique woman who was never convinced of her "enoughness."

Death—whether our own impending passing or that of someone close to us—has a way of revealing what we hope for, distilling what we truly believe. Often, a loved one's death becomes a doorway to new life for those who remain; it's difficult to stay the same after grieving someone dear to you.

For me, saying good-bye to Gigi brought this question to the fore: How does my view of eternity shape the way I live today? Will eternal life simply be a relief for me—no more disease, no more tears, no more sin—or is there something more to hope for and expect? Christ's words in John 11 offer specific truths about life everlasting:

> I am the resurrection and the life. The one who believes in me will live, even though they die; and whoever lives by believing in me will never die. Do you believe this? (vv. 25–26)

The When, Where, and Why

When we approach any passage of Scripture, it's essential that we explore its context: to whom were these words directed? When, where, and why were they spoken? Because a fundamental understanding of context must inform our interpretation and application of biblical truth, we will devote the first portion of each remaining chapter to evaluating the context within which Jesus makes his great "I am" claims.

John 11:1–44 recounts a single tale, a story of loss and grief, redemption and resurrection. In this chapter, we're reintroduced to

Mary and Martha, sisters who figure prominently in Jesus's life and other Gospel accounts. Their brother, Lazarus, has fallen gravely ill, and the sisters send word to Jesus: "Lord, the one you love is sick." Christ responds to the messengers, "This sickness will not end in death. No, it is for God's glory so that God's Son may be glorified through it" (John 11:3, 4). So far so good, it would seem.

Jesus stays where he is another two days, then tells his disciples it's time to head to Bethany, where Lazarus lies ill. Answering the "When?" and "Where?" of this passage becomes essential here. Jesus had recently been in Jerusalem for the Feast of Dedication. While there, the religious leaders accused Jesus of blasphemy, attempting to seize and stone him, "but he escaped their grasp" (John 10:39). When Jesus told his disciples they were going to Bethany, only a few miles from Jerusalem, they must have been confused. Why would they go back there, where certain death awaited? He had already told them that Lazarus wouldn't die; his sickness would result in God's glory. Did the disciples wonder if God's glory had to come at the price of their safety?

The story takes a curious turn when Jesus arrives in Bethany. Lazarus is not only dead, he's been in the tomb four days. The disciples find Martha and Mary wracked with grief, surrounded by wailing friends. So far, *no good*. Death and suffering pervade Bethany, and as Jesus draws close to her home, Martha runs to meet him.

"Lord," Martha laments, "if you had been here, my brother would not have died. But I know that even now God will give you whatever you ask."

Jesus replies with tenderness: "Your brother will rise again."

Martha answers with a solid, Sunday-school-type answer: "I know he will rise again in the resurrection at the last day."

Jesus affirms that as true, but reveals much more as well: "I am the resurrection and the life. The one who believes in me will live, even though they die; and whoever lives by believing in me will never die. Do you believe this?" (see John 11:21–26).

We must not overlook that when Jesus speaks these words, it's to a cherished friend. The text makes clear: "Now Jesus loved Martha and her sister and Lazarus" (John 11:5). These aren't merely theological statements. He speaks to Martha's grieving heart, and his words echo in our hearts today. "I am the resurrection and the life" juxtaposes our utter helplessness in the face of death with the transcendent power of God, from whom all life flows.

It's important to remember that when Jesus makes this claim, neither Martha nor Mary knows what is to come. As modern readers, we forget that Christ's statement may have seemed only a promise of *future* truth to the heartbroken sisters: "Of course, Lord; we know Lazarus will rise again on the last day," Martha responds. This, however, is not how the story ends; Jesus reveals he is God in the *present* tense.

Mary and Martha take Jesus to Lazarus's tomb, where he grieves with them, weeping with compassion and understanding. Our Lord knows what it's like to stand at a graveside! The Greek word used in John 11:33 indicates Christ was literally "shaken" with heartache, deeply troubled by the agony confronting him. Jesus doesn't dismiss our emotion and suffering in the face of death; instead he fulfills the biblical promise, "He took up our infirmities and bore our diseases" (Matt. 8:17). John 11 shows us that Jesus *felt* the burden of sin, pain, and death before he removed it.

And remove it he does! First he asks those surrounding him to participate in the miracle to come. "Take away the stone," he commands. Because Martha reacts with horror—"Lord, think of the smell!"—Jesus next confronts the unbelief that lurks at every graveside and in every heart: "Did I not tell you that if you believe, you will see the glory of God?" Directing his eyes heavenward, Jesus thanks God for hearing him and caring for the people of earth. The story climaxes as Jesus cries in a loud and triumphant voice, "Lazarus, come out!" His beloved friend, walking away from the grave and very much alive, provides proof of Jesus's exalted claim. *Life* has the last word.

The Same Power

"I am the resurrection and the life; he who believes in me will never die." I used to sing a chorus with those words at youth group. I remember there was a lot of clapping involved and a generally celebratory tone; it was the kind of song I loved as a girl because I felt so *alive* singing it. Unfortunately, I skimmed only the surface of the powerful truths I memorized and sang. Perhaps I didn't listen well enough when my pastor spoke on this topic, but for a good deal of my life, I viewed Jesus's words in John 11 primarily as a promise of future hope. Even though I parroted, "I *am* the resurrection and the life," I thought Jesus's real point was, "I *will be* the resurrection and life for you . . . when you die."

I viewed eternal life as a destination, somewhere I would go when this earthly life was over. I don't recall being taught that eternal life was actually a *culmination* of the new life begun when I said yes to Jesus. Christ looks at immortality in a vastly different way than I comprehended. I love how the *Expositor's Bible* commentary articulates this transforming truth: Jesus defines eternal life "not as a future continuance to be measured by ages, but as a present life, to be measured by its depth. It is the quality, not the length, of life He looks at."[1]

Eternal life is about quality, not just quantity? Everlasting life is more about *source* than longevity? It's a *present-tense* reality? Yes! In the words of Henri Nouwen, "Eternal life is not some great surprise that comes unannounced at the end of our existence in time; it is, rather, the full revelation of what we have been and have lived all along."[2]

What would the full revelation of what I have been and have lived all along look like? Am I living a resurrection life *now*? I slowly came to grips with a rather startling reality: my gospel had a gaping hole in the middle. I spoke with some level of understanding and certainly a great deal of gratitude about the forgiveness of my sin, accomplished by Jesus on the cross. I looked forward with anticipation and joy to life with him in heaven, but the *nowism* of the gospel—the present tense of my eternal life—was strikingly absent.[3]

Jesus is the Resurrection and the Life, our present and unceasing life, the life that will continue through eternity. This "I Am" statement makes clear that immortality is always tied to life, life as a present thing, as a full, abundant, and glad experience. The same power that raised Jesus from the grave is at work in us and through us today, right this instant.

Death cuts across many things: our dreams, hopes, and aspirations. It drags destruction and heartache along with it. But for Christians, neither physical death nor the disappointment of expectations and dreams is the end of the story. Ever. When you choose Jesus, life *always* has the final word. Our great hope lies not only in the truth that death does not have the final word in an ultimate sense, but that in our present life, no story is entirely finished. Do you believe it?

When Martha and Jesus spoke of resurrection, she referred to a conviction that "at the last day" her brother would rise again. Biblical scholars tie her words to a verse in Job, where the suffering servant of God declares, "I know that my redeemer lives, and that in the end he will stand on the earth" (Job 19:25). The beautiful promise of this passage is both for that day when Christ will reign victorious, but also for *this day*. Why? Because Jesus is the present-tense Redeemer of whom Job spoke. "Redeemer" means, in essence, "the One who gives me back my life." Jesus will not merely resuscitate you on the last day; he is *currently* at work, redeeming you. He *is* the Resurrection and the Life.

Resuscitation is all about restoring a former life, bringing someone back to what they've known. Redemption and resurrection are about something far more glorious: rebirth into an entirely new life, an eternal life where everything—even death—works together for the good of those called according to his purpose (see Rom. 8:28).

Bodily death is merely the symptom of a deeper disease: alienation from God as the result of sin, and thereby separation from all that is good, true, and beautiful in this world and the next. The real danger from which Christ delivers us is life apart from God. This is why Jesus is not merely the Resurrection, but also *the Life*.

When Christ proclaims he is the Resurrection and the Life, he invites us to something new, and new can often translate to "unnerving" in our minds. When we're confronted with change or the need for transformation, we often default to a "What is this gonna take?" mind-set.

Most Christian women I interact with crave this kind of "practical application." They want to know "how to" live the life Christ died to give them. Being of a pragmatic, worker-bee temperament myself, I completely understand this. The trouble is, it doesn't work to look at "how to" without first looking at what's in the way. The best instructor in the world cannot help my teenage daughters learn to drive on a road strewn with two-ton boulders. The obstacles must be removed before the "how to" makes any sense.

In a similar way, the things preventing us from living a present-tense resurrection life must first be acknowledged and eradicated before we can apply tips and techniques. Indeed, we often discover that, once the hindrances to our faith are removed, we find running the race of faith easier and lighter than we imagined (see Heb. 12:1–2). Two of the greatest saboteurs of our resurrection life are fear and shame.

Like razor-sharp thorns, the powerful emotions that come with fear and shame prick us painfully. Instead of dealing with the thorns (the shame and fear), however, we often focus on making the uncomfortable emotions go away. We compensate for, rearrange, and manage our behavior so we won't hurt. As individuals, we do this in unique ways, tailored over years of experience to fit our personality and proclivities. Most of us don't want to lean into pain and discover what it means or where it might lead. Instead, we take the edge off with work, binge watching, web surfing, control, caring for others, busyness, relationships, shopping, perfectionism, or physical pleasure (from food, alcohol, sex, etc.). If we are to live the present-tense resurrection life Christ offers us, however, we must get to the root of our problem, the shameful and fearful thought patterns that keep us in bondage.

Should You Be Ashamed of Yourself?

Shame is a universal and primal emotion, one that leaves us with emotional distress and physical symptoms to boot: dry mouth, tunnel vision, hot face, racing heart, the sense of time grinding to slow motion, every failure you've ever known looping in your brain. Shame is similar to what I feel when I try to edit a picture on my computer. Even a shot I like decently well turns into a horror story on tight zoom. Every flaw and imperfection, focused in sharp relief, causes me to lose joy in the bigger picture. Shame also isolates me from others—no one can see me this way!—and causes me to hide. I bet you know just what I'm talking about. Nearly every woman I've met or corresponded with knows something of shame, the kind that steals resurrection life from within us.

In his masterwork, *Shame and Grace*, theologian Lewis Smedes defines shame brilliantly: "Shame is a very heavy feeling. It is a feeling that we do not measure up and maybe never will measure up to the sorts of persons we are meant to be. The feeling, when we are conscious of it, gives us a vague disgust with ourselves, which in turn feels like a hunk of lead on our hearts."[4] This ambiguous, undefined heaviness weighs on the spirit, dulls our awareness of and gratitude for goodness in life, and blocks the flow of joy in our hearts. When left unchecked, shame seeps into every thought and relationship, discoloring our experience and emotions, ultimately attaching to our minds a dead weight of "not-good-enoughness."

Shame adds to this heaviness a nagging suspicion that if people truly knew us—our "real" selves—they would find us wanting and therefore unlovable. Because shame deceives us into believing ourselves unworthy, it prevents us from trusting in our belovedness to God and others. Indeed, the fundamental lie at work in shame is this: *Flawed people don't belong and don't deserve love.* It's easy to see why shame has been called a soul-eating emotion. Shame literally devours you from the inside out.

Author and researcher Brené Brown has spent more than a decade researching shame. She discovered "shame corrodes the part of us that believes we can change and do better." To do this, Brown reveals, "shame needs three things to grow out of control in our lives: secrecy, silence, and judgment."[5] Though most of us are afraid to talk about the heavy weight of our not-good-enoughness, the more we hide or deny, the more shame exerts its wretched control over our lives. Brown continues, "The very best thing to do when this is happening feels totally counterintuitive: Practice courage and reach out! . . . Shame hates having words wrapped around it—it can't survive being shared. Shame loves secrecy. The most dangerous thing to do after a shaming experience is hide or bury our story. When we bury our story, the shame metastasizes."[6]

To stem the toxic flow of shame, we can use words of truth as both a weapon and a shield. When confronted with shame—a sense that you are not and never will be the person you're "supposed" to be—lean into what God has said about you: you are precious, honored, and beloved. Shame cannot stand being brought into the light of his Word.

It also cannot remain when people acknowledge one another's weaknesses and choose to love instead of judge. Shame happens between people and it must be healed between them too.[7] According to Dr. Linda Hartling, another shame researcher, people respond to shame in three ways: they either (1) *move away* from others by withdrawing, hiding, and/or silencing themselves; (2) *move toward* others, seeking to please and appease; or (3) *move against* others, using aggression to exert control, with an "I'll make sure you don't like me so you can't hurt me" mind-set.[8]

From a strictly earthly perspective, these reactions make sense. We see the fruit of people's choices in this realm every day: isolation, aggression, or viral people-pleasing based on a fear of being exposed or "found out" plague many women. Is there a better way? Yes, but we'll have to wade through the swampland of fear before we can get there.

The Terrible Trio

We cannot overcome shame without discussing fear because fear is a master emotion, a controller of motive, action, and speech. Fear of disappointing people or being found wanting and unlovable is what fuels shame, so the two are inseparable, if unwelcome, companions on our life journey.

Because fear doesn't look the same in each of our lives, this is a complex issue. Many women would hesitate to deem themselves *fearful*, but chronic, low-level worry? Well, that's a different matter! Isn't worrying just part of being a woman? For others, fear seems a mild word; the anxiety they face is gripping both physically and emotionally; it holds the spirit hostage as well.

Fear, worry, and anxiety are a terrible trio sharing common origin and expression. And, in an interesting twist, most of our battles with this terrible trio stem from the anticipation of another threesome: loss, rejection, and failure.[9]

We worry about losing our loved ones, position, the respect of others. We're anxious not to miss opportunities or surrender freedoms, and these concerns motivate choices, good and bad. We're afraid both that some people have already rejected us and that others will turn their backs on us if "this" or "that" happens. And we're desperately worried that we have failed, will fail—or are failing at this very moment—in our education, careers, parenting, etc. I don't have to enumerate all the worries we face as women. Most of us go to bed with one or two and wake up with the same or a whole new set. Psychologists have even come up with a phrase for the kind of worry women face—*meta worry*, the worry about worrying. Isn't that the sad truth?!

I used to think that if I was just a good enough Christian, I'd be able to get rid of the terrible trio of fear, anxiety, and worry. I now understand that, because this world has been broken by sin and therefore doesn't operate the way God originally designed it to function, worries will keep cropping up. Like most everything else, it's what you and I *do* with these triggers, *how we respond* to them that shapes our lives. I spent many years trying to banish the terrible trio. Now I focus my energies on laying the concerns down. Instead of beating myself up for getting into bed with my thoughts whirling—once again!—I take the opportunity to acknowledge to God where I am (*Lord, these things are weighing me down*), thank him for what he's done to shoulder the weight of my worry (*I am so grateful I don't have to figure this out alone!*), and claim what he's promised (*Jesus, you've told me if I surrender my cares to you, you will grant me peace that goes beyond what I can understand. I receive that now, by your grace*).

It's also been incredibly important for me to identify specific ways the terrible trio creep into my mind. For me, it's mostly through "what-ifs" and "if onlys." And wouldn't you know it? Mary and Martha faced these troubles as they grieved their brother's death: "*If* you had been here, Lazarus wouldn't have died," the sisters lamented. In the words of A. W. Pink, "This was the language of perplexity and grief. Like Martha, Mary was thinking of what might have happened. How often we look back on the past with an 'if' in our minds! How often in our sore trials we lash ourselves with an 'if.' And small comfort does it bring! How often we complain 'it might have been.' . . . As Whittier says, 'Of all sad words of tongue and pen, the saddest are these, 'It might have been.'"[10]

How often we lash ourselves. This vivid language fits well with my experience of the terrible trio of fear, worry, and anxiety. Most of my worries never come to pass, but the lashing I give myself as I consider them is pain enough! Perhaps, like me, you've observed that many fears are unjustified and, though it's somewhat embarrassing to admit, pretty insubstantial; there's no gravity to them because "if onlys" and "what-ifs" aren't *real*. They're imaginations that we allow to run wild, somewhat like Maurice Sendak's monsters in *Where the Wild Things Are*. Our worries and fears "gnash their terrible teeth, roar their terrible roars and show their terrible claws," but it's all an illusion. Usually, rather than the quality of our fears, it's the sheer *quantity* of them that overwhelms us.

There are, of course, crippling fears that are *very real*, and we should not dismiss those with a biblical Band-Aid: "Well, just leave your worries with God and it'll all be okay." (If this were a text message, I imagine some well-meaning friend inserting an annoying prayer emoji here.) When you receive a cancer diagnosis, when your child is caught with drugs at school, or when your husband has been out of work for more than a year, the fears don't feel like illusions anymore. Even in these moments, my beloved sister in Christ, *even in these what-ifs and if onlys*, we don't know what the future holds. No matter what your doctor says, what the principal or counselor or book on the subject claims, however grim the outlook is, there is only One who holds life and resurrection in his hands. He can bring back what is dead—a careening career, an ailing body, a broken relationship, a rebellious teenager. He *is* the Resurrection and the Life.

I'll be honest with you: the difficulty for me comes not in "believing" this but in actively surrendering my desire to know all and control all. I affectionately refer to myself as a "recovering control freak" because I have battled long and hard with an inordinate fear of losing control.

We all develop coping strategies to combat the terrible trio, and control is the default choice for lots of women. Many of us continually operate on a fundamental lie: outward order leads to peace of mind. Don't be fooled, as I have too often been! When trials reveal that we have very little (if any) control over our circumstances, our faith can be shaken. Why? Because it has been placed in the wrong thing. Ironically, fear of losing control begins to control you: where you go, with whom you build friendships, what you do and why. If you trust no one's plans but your own, if you have only your own strength and resources on which to depend, anything that happens "off" your agenda is a crisis of great magnitude. This is bondage!

Through a trial of horrific proportions—an extended battle with mental illness that began with postpartum depression— I began to long for freedom from the tyranny of "what-ifs" and "if onlys," the fears that compelled me to freeze, faint, fight, or flee. The shame of being mentally ill haunted me. In that brokenness, I also became *desperate* for the presence of God in a way I had never experienced.

Slowly, gently, lovingly, he pried my shaking hands from the steering wheel of life. Worry, fear, and anxiety—that terrible trio— had never been banished by my resolve anyway. They hadn't gone away just because someone told me not to be afraid. Reading Scripture hadn't magically alleviated fear, because hearing and knowing a truth is not enough. I needed to *rightly apply* that truth by the grace of God; my daily life needed to be reordered. Remember, just because you've rejected a wrong thought does not mean that you have embraced a right one. To experience genuine freedom in Christ, you cannot white-knuckle your way to right belief. You must *actively choose* to trust in God and ask him to transform your life with his thoughts, his truth, and habits that honor him.

One of my absolute favorite verses is Jeremiah 32:17: "Ah, Sovereign Lord, you have made the heavens and the earth by your great power and outstretched arm. Nothing is too hard for you." Sadly, "too often we conclude that if a thing is beyond our control or power to act, then it is also beyond God's. Many of our prayers include instructions to God on how to naturally meet our requests using means open to *our* disposal. . . . Our God who is able to speak light into darkness and create out of nothing is able to work in every circumstance that life presents."[11] *Nothing is too hard for your sovereign Lord.* Allow me to ask, as Jesus did when he walked this earth, "Do you believe this?"

The terrible trio may threaten us, but we have the same power living in us that raised Lazarus and, even more significantly, Jesus himself from the grave. I just read in my quiet time today a verse from Colossians 1. I'm sure I've come across it many times before, but it struck me anew this morning, knowing that I would be writing this chapter: "And this is the secret: Christ lives in you. This gives you assurance of sharing his glory" (1:27 NLT). *Christ lives in you.* Don't let this marvelous truth pass you by because you've heard it before. Resurrection and life are living in you—right now, present tense—and the terrible trio has no power over you that you do not give it.

Removing the Marks of the Grave

If given power in a woman's life, fear and shame can actually steal the place of God in her heart. They can become the cornerstone of her identity and the default mode of her thinking, speaking, and action. Both fear and shame are tyrants. They are not content with small corners of your life; they aim at domination and complete control. Fear and shame want to become your all-consuming passion. They can only be replaced by a stronger, more enduring love.

As we've observed, resurrection is not merely about resuscitating a life that has been lost; it's an invitation to live differently. This is an invasive process, and one that's not always welcomed. Some women are more comfortable with their shame and their fears than with resurrection life. They've adapted to their worries, made allowances for their shame for so long that living a new life actually seems threatening. Resurrection life meddles with everything they've known. It offers peace to a mind that's trained itself to worry and confidence to a soul that's staked its claim in the swampland of shame; living in truth feels foreign and uncomfortable. Bottom line, we have to *want* to get well in order to overcome fear and shame. We must believe there is something better for us.

After Jesus called Lazarus out of the tomb, John 11:44 tells us, "The dead man came out, his hands and feet wrapped with strips of linen, and a cloth around his face. Jesus said to them, 'Take off the grave clothes and let him go.'"

When Jesus resurrects us, whether in the moment of our conversion or from a death-like experience in life, the marks of the grave need removing. Fear and shame may cling like grave clothes to the believer's flesh, but resurrection life is the truth of her identity.

In an amazing, only-God-can-make-this-happen way, it's possible to view shame and fear as allies in our sanctification; they actually can lead us to seek Christ more fervently! *Our choices determine whether shame and fear control us or compel us to holiness.* Saying no to shame and fear shows the true value we place on the gospel of peace. Living resurrection life means trusting that he will overcome, not just on the final day, but in the here and now (and in his best way).

I love the simplicity with which Jeanne Guyon wrote of this in the seventeenth century: "What does a little child do when he sees something that frightens him or confuses him?" she asks. "He doesn't stand there and try to fight the thing. He will, in fact, hardly look at the thing that frightens him. Rather, the child will quickly run into the arms of his mother. . . . In exactly the same way, you should turn from the dangers of temptation and *run* to your God. . . . If you attempt to struggle directly with these temptations, you will only strengthen them; and in the process of this struggle, your soul will be drawn away from its intimate relationship with the Lord."[12]

Some of you did not grow up knowing the comfort or safety of a parent's love. If you were to run to your father or mother, you might have been laughed at or dismissed, ignored or scolded.

Such is never the case with your loving heavenly Father. According to Romans 8:14–15, he is our Abba—the perfect Daddy—the one who protects you from the fears that haunt and the shame that plagues. You are accepted, received, and cherished by him.

Both the temptations presented by the terrible trio of worry, fear, and anxiety, as well as the temptation to get mired in shame, can be overcome only by running to your loving, perfect Lord. Like Mary and Martha, we must remember that whether faced with sickness of body or sickness of heart and mind, we are to call on Christ and *know* him—not merely cognitively, but also experientially—in the power of his resurrection life (Phil. 3:10).

When we know and center our lives on Christ, hopeful living moves from the realm of activity to incarnation. That means hope springs up within us, giving us the strength, courage, and power we need when the burdens of life feel insupportable and the battles too fierce to fight. Because Jesus has conquered the final enemy, death, none of its earthly powers—pain, fear, shame, etc.—can cast more than a shadow over us (Ps. 23:4).

One of the best ways to practice knowing Christ in the power of his life and resurrection is somewhat counterintuitive. At least it seemed that way to me when I first encountered the idea. Practicing the prayer of gratitude removes the marks of the grave more than anything else. Rather than engaging directly with our fears and shame, thanksgiving empowers us to overcome them.

Practicing the Prayer of Gratitude

After my battle with postpartum depression, I began studying neuroscience. I discovered that it was a wonderful source of comfort and worship for me. As I understood what was happening in my (very broken) brain, I was able to surrender my physical struggles to Jesus and also do what he asked me to do to maintain my resurrected health.

In the process, God taught me some amazing things about the brain, incredibly practical things I could apply right away. One of these things concerned the relationship between fear, shame, and gratitude.

When you and I experience worry, anxiety, fear, and shame, toxic chemicals flood our brain and move into our bloodstream. This explains, in part, why we physically experience symptoms like rapid heartbeat, sour stomach pain, headaches, etc., when confronted with negative emotions.

Neurologist Dr. Caroline Leaf explains, "Research shows that fear triggers more than 1,400 known physical and chemical responses and activates more than 30 different hormones and neurotransmitters! While they may originate externally, all stressors eventually become internal because everything you see, hear and feel becomes part of your thought life."[13]

Toxic thoughts associated with worry and shame travel along very specific brain highways. Here's what's radical: these pathways and those for gratitude are mutually exclusive. From a physiological standpoint, you *cannot* be anxious and grateful at the same moment. It is, quite literally, impossible. If you'd like to see the scientific evidence for this, check out the endnote.[14]

This should come as no surprise to us, considering what Jesus commanded us through the apostle Paul: "Don't worry about anything; instead, pray about everything. Tell God what you need, and thank him for all he has done. Then you will experience God's peace, which exceeds anything we can understand. His peace will guard your hearts and minds as you live in Christ Jesus" (Phil. 4:6–7 NLT).

Thousands of years before neuroscientists discovered it, our God gave us the most powerful weapon we need to fight shame and the terrible trio: gratitude. He also displayed this practice in his own life and ministry. If you read through the Gospel accounts, you'll find that every miracle Jesus performed was preceded by an expression of thanksgiving.

Think of it this way: gratitude removes the stone and the grave clothes so you can enjoy resurrection life. Gratitude is what we can *do* to participate in Jesus's resurrection power.

And the wonderful thing about giving thanks is that it's not circumstance-specific. You don't have to conjure up gratitude for the situation you're facing or fearing. Instead of trying to white-knuckle a "Thank you, Lord, for this hardship and what you'll do through it," start with a simple prayer for something you're grateful for every day. For me, salted caramel mochas and peanut butter are always go-tos. Sunshine and the sound of waves too. Practicing the prayer of gratitude rolls away the stones of fear and shame in my life, and it can in your life too. Don't just take my word for it; trust the Great Physician who designed your brain and loves your heart!

Why not take a moment and practice the prayer of gratitude by coming up with five things—no matter how small—that you are thankful for? Here's another challenge: next time a worry threatens to overtake you, try praying five things you're grateful for. You may find that stopping whatever you're doing and saying them out loud is most effective. As you incorporate this habit into your day-to-day activities, his resurrection life will empower you and overflow into the lives of those around you as well.

Hallelujah! The same power that raised Jesus from the grave lives in us!

~~~

Questions for Personal Reflection or Group Discussion

1. Journal about or discuss the following: "Eternal life is not some great surprise that comes unannounced at the end of our existence in time; it is, rather, the full revelation of what we have been and have lived all along." What would the full

revelation of what you have been and have lived all along look like?

2. How have shame and the terrible trio of worry, fear, and anxiety weighed on you in the past? How do they impact you today?

3. Stop and practice the prayer of gratitude on your own or with your group. Encourage your friends to practice it whenever you hear them use shameful or worry-filled words.

Recommended Reading

- Brown, Brené. *The Gifts of Imperfection: Let Go of Who You Think You're Supposed to Be and Embrace Who You Are*. Center City, MN: Hazelden Publishing, 2010.
- Smedes, Lewis. *Shame and Grace: Healing the Shame We Don't Deserve*. New York: HarperCollins, 1993.

{4}

You're Always In

"I'm just sick of being the least important person at the table."

My remarkably perceptive teenage daughter sighed heavily, tossed her backpack in the trunk of our Explorer, and slammed the passenger door. Though I'm a woman accustomed to using words to sort out my thoughts and feelings, though I'd taught my daughters to make sense of life with words from the time they began uttering sounds, in this instance I was struck utterly dumb.

My vibrant, intelligent girl . . . the least important person at the lunch table? Why? How? Where can I get hold of these foolish teenage girls who are hurting my baby? And why in the world did memories of being picked last, not getting invited to that party, and overhearing whispering "friends" who quickly stopped talking when I walked up swim into my consciousness? Wasn't I over all that nonsense?

I picked my other daughter up from middle school some time later. Hot tears glistened in her blue eyes. When I asked, "Is there something wrong?" I got the immediate "It's nothing . . ." response.

Not buying it, I pressed in: "Please tell me what happened . . ."

That's all it took to burst the dam of tears and tension.

"Savannah doesn't even talk to me, Mom. Every day she says hi and gives a hug to everyone else in our group, but she acts like I don't even exist. I'm already on the outside because I don't play soccer. I don't know why she doesn't like me. It's like I'm invisible and it just hurts . . . a lot."

I wished so much I could take away my daughters' pain. I hoped I could give them some encouragement. I knew I could pray for and with them. I absolutely trusted that God would walk them through these heartaches, just as he had done with me through the agonizing years of adolescence. At the same time, I was uncomfortably aware of one thing I could not do—tell them that it would be totally different when they became adults.

Women can be downright mean. And I'm not excluding Christian ladies from that statement. Some of the most exclusive cliques I've come across are those in Bible study and church circles. There's nothing quite like being rejected by women who claim to love "the least of these."

To some extent, you and I and *all people* yearn for acceptance and approval. Some mask this desire with a gruff, "I couldn't care less" exterior; others numb it by being cold and cruel. But most of us, and women almost invariably more so than our male counterparts, spend exorbitant amounts of time and energy trying to make relationships work.

I used to believe that wanting to fit in was strictly a negative thing. As a Christian, I reasoned, only God's opinion should matter; what other people think should have no bearing on how I feel or what I do. While there is wisdom in thoughts like these, the truth is more complex than this kind of "all or nothing" paradigm allows.

God created us for relationship, both with him and with others. Fellowship is an eternal reality designed by our loving Father, an original glory that predates the fall. When I cross over, I will not be in an individual heaven populated only by the Holy Trinity and myself; neither will you. Instead, we will dwell forever in perfect unity with people from every tribe and every nation. Every single one of us will be eternally "in." If you ask me, that sounds pretty good. Jesus said, "I am the gate; whoever enters through me will be saved. They will come in and go out, and find pasture" (John 10:9).

The When, Where, and Why

Jesus speaks these words after performing a miracle that incensed some and amazed others. In John 9, he heals a man born blind. Furious at Jesus's rising popularity and undeniable power, the religious leaders vow "that anyone who acknowledged that Jesus was the Messiah would be put out of the synagogue" (John 9:22).

The Greek word used here, *aposynagōgos*, is a compound verb connoting excommunication. Don't imagine this means, "You can't come to church here; try the one two miles away." This term indicates *absolute exclusion* from the social and spiritual fellowship of the community. "Cast out," "cut off," and "abandoned" would be appropriate synonyms. To these people, at this moment, Jesus declares, "I am the door; if anyone enters through Me, he will be saved, and will go in and out and find pasture" (John 10:9 NASB). In essence, Jesus told the excluders and haters, "You cannot stand in the way. I *am* the way in, and whoever I receive has complete access, total freedom."

To every woman who has been on the outside, anyone who's felt rejected and judged, Jesus proclaims today, "With me, you're always *in*. Come; find freedom in me. Be strengthened by what I provide and go back out into the world, confident in who I've made you to be. You may come back in any time you like, for the door is always open to those who are mine."

All-Access Security

Certain buildings distinguish themselves with marble columns and intricate molding. Some boast unusual paint jobs or striking architecture. Unique doors identify still others.

When Jesus describes himself as "the door" or "the gate"[1] in John 10:9, he speaks of a unique point of access, the way of admittance to our true home, in the presence of God our Father. Through this door—Jesus alone—can we receive salvation; through him only can we find unconditional belonging, security, and shelter. He is not "a" door that may or may not lead where you hope; Jesus is unequivocally *the* Door that provides access to everlasting life and hope.

And what wonderfully open access it is! Theologian A. W. Pink describes it well: "There are no difficult walls which have to be scaled before the anxious sinner can obtain access to God. No, Christ is the 'door' into His presence. A 'door' may . . . be contrasted from a long, dreary, circuitous passage—just one step, and those on the outside are now within. The soul that believes God's testimony to the truth of salvation by Christ alone, at once enters God's presence."[2] Imagine! Just one step and you have crossed over from death to life, from fear to freedom.

This is what Jesus, the Living Door, yearns to provide for us: not a long, dreary, circuitous passage of religiosity, but an instant welcome into the arms of our loving, forgiving Father. How tragic that so many make the walk of faith the exact opposite of what God intended. Too many women lumber down dead-end hallways of self-righteousness or shame, striving to climb high walls of performance and perfectionism. The door is open, but we must choose to walk through it. There is no other way.

Beyond simple points of entrance, doors also separate spaces and offer safety for those who take shelter behind them. The need for security was something the Hebrews to whom Jesus spoke would have instantly understood. Jesus's claim, "I am the door" is nestled in his larger parable of the Good Shepherd (John 10:1–10), an important fact considering the cultural context of ancient Palestine, where neighbors often shared a common sheepfold.

Each evening, shepherds would bring their flocks into a community enclosure—sometimes formed of natural barriers like large rocks, other times built with walls ten to twelve feet high—to protect the sheep from wild predators and cunning thieves. An opening on one side of the sheepfold was fixed with a gate or primitive door. Other times, a shepherd or porter "became" the door, laying his body across the opening of the sheepfold, fencing in the sheep and assuring their sanctuary with his own physical presence. If beast or bandit came near, the shepherd-door would defend the sheep, often to his own peril. Jesus's words, "I am the gate" speak of his willingness to lay down his life for us. He is our Living Door, aware of and on guard against every threatening circumstance in our lives. This is a promise of *absolute* security. Isn't it marvelous?

As I noted earlier, doors also separate spaces. While Jesus, as God's door, openly offers salvation to all, we must choose to enter through him. Tragically, so many people are desperate for belonging and freedom, yet they continue to knock at the wrong door. They look to relationships (and women like us sometimes turn first to friends, a spouse, or our children) for comfort and a sense of security. While we may not go quite as far as to look to other people to "save" us, we're often knocking on the wrong door for acceptance and contentment.

In John 10:9, Jesus also indicates a separation between "in" and "out." His sheep "will come in and go out, and find pasture." This perplexed me. If going "in" means that I am eternally saved and accepted, why would I ever go "out"? How could I "find pasture" away from Christ? These were questions I needed answers to, so I studied the text more intently.

In this context, Jesus refers not to leaving his presence, but rather to the separation between our interior and exterior lives of faith. Philip Keller, who spent many years as a shepherd before becoming a pastor, helped me understand this: A literal sheep flock "has both an interior life within the shelter of the sheepfold and an exterior life outside. It is by means of the doorway, through the opening of the gate, that they enjoy both ingress and egress to a fully rounded and beneficial mode of life." Just so, in the Christian life, we have an interior life of the soul and an exterior life lived with others. Keller continues, "As we come to rely implicitly upon . . . His laid-down life and spilled blood, [Jesus] becomes the doorway for us. It is through Him that we enjoy a magnificent inner security and through Him that we go out to engage in an adventurous life of new-found freedom under His direction."[3]

Christ's declaration that we will go in and out offers us a beautiful picture of perfect freedom. Timid sheep might want to stay in the sheepfold day and night, but in doing so, they would miss the glorious pastures on the outside. Hardheaded, arrogant ewes might want to stay out all night, but doing so exposes them to dangers of every kind. In a similar manner, we need the security, rest, and intimacy of a deep interior life with Jesus *and* the adventure, exercise, and challenge of life on the outside, an exterior life of faith that includes being with others. Both joys and sorrows come with that.

Friendship Would Be Great . . . If It Weren't for People

In 1944, C. S. Lewis gave a lecture called "The Inner Ring." He claimed, "I believe that in all [lives] . . . one of the most dominant elements is the desire to be inside the local Ring and the terror of being left outside."[4]

We all know the draw of an "inner ring," whether at our workplace, school, church, or even within our extended family. The inner ring is the group(s) we aspire to be part of, whether simply for the security of being "in" or, more complexly, for the position, identity, and value we think we'll enjoy once admitted.

Groups are not inherently evil; their insidious nature arises as the "inner ring" plays on our hearts. It's the futility and the pain of *striving* for acceptance that introduces what Lewis called a "pell-mell of struggle, competition, confusion, graft, disappointment and advertisement." He warned,

Unless you take measures to prevent it, this desire is going to be one of the chief motives of your life, from the first day . . . until the day when you are too old to care. That will be the natural thing—the life that will come to you of its own accord. Any other kind of life, if you lead it, will be the result of conscious and continuous effort. If you do nothing about it, if you drift with the stream, you will in fact be an "inner ringer." I don't say you'll be a successful one; that's as may be. But whether by pining and moping outside Rings that you can never enter, or by passing triumphantly further and further in—one way or the other you will be that kind of [person].[5]

I don't want to be that kind of woman.

It will take a conscious and continuous effort for me to avoid the draw of the "inner ring," however. The same is true for you. This is where Jesus's promise, "I am the gate; whoever enters through me . . . will come in and go out, and find pasture," must become a living word, defining our heart motivations and the actions that spring from them.

If you and I are forever "in" with Jesus and our acceptance cannot be revoked, when we go "out" into the world and interact with all manner of people—some of whom *will* despise and reject us—we can remain secure in our belovedness and approval. Do you see how being forever accepted by God changes *everything*? You are in with Jesus—*always in*—and no one can take that away.

With all my heart, I encourage you each and every day to first "go in" to the rest and peace found in Jesus alone. Go into his presence with holy boldness in prayer (Heb. 4:15). Go in to him as a beloved daughter and adopted heiress. Go in, that the light of his face may shine upon you and give you peace (Num. 6:24–26).

I also urge you then to go out in the perfect liberty of your Lord. Go out, trusting in Christ as you go about your everyday business. Go out through Christ, the door, rather than blundering out to face the world on your own. When you go out, confident of your acceptance in Jesus, you don't relate to others from a place of weakness, from an emptiness aching to be filled. Instead, you go out saying, "Lord, I am Yours. I don't know what may happen, but I am going out in Your name and resting in Your strength."[6] What could you possibly lose by trying this? What could you gain? Do you think your relationships might be different if you truly believed that you were already fully in?

Breaking the Bonds of Bitterness

Trusting completely in our unshakable "in"ness, our acceptance and belovedness in Jesus, frees us from envy and bitterness, all-too-frequent barriers to relationships.

Sad to say, women (myself included) often fall prey to unforgiveness and resentment, whether manifested through aggressive outbursts, stony silence, vicious gossip, or depressed resignation. Indeed, I have found that forgiveness is more often than not *the* issue, not "an" issue for women with wounded hearts and broken relationships. I've spent a good deal of my ministry researching and writing about bitterness and forgiveness. I've focused on this topic both because of its centrality for women in general, and also because I need—each and every day—to be reminded that my security and acceptance in Jesus means I can bravely face the hurts done to me and those I've inflicted upon others.[7]

Because I am forever "in" with Jesus and have been forgiven of more than I could *ever possibly* be asked to forgive (see Matt. 18:21–35), I can remember redemptively and live freely. Redemptive remembering is a practice I first came across in the work of Lewis Smedes, whose books on forgiveness are two of my absolute favorites.[8] Remembering redemptively follows the pattern of Genesis 50:20, in which Joseph declared to the brothers who betrayed him: "You intended to harm me, but God intended it for good to accomplish what is now being done, the saving of many lives."

When you and I choose to forgive, we don't forget what happened. Nor do we dismiss it, minimize it, or let the "other guy" off the hook. Instead, we actively choose to remember differently. We can choose to focus on what God intended—the *good* he either has brought or the hope of what he will bring out of wrongs, whether trifling or terrifying ones.

Some of the wounds you've faced may be so egregious you can't fathom how God might use them for good. Abuse, racism, and rape are among the most horrific wrongs women can experience. There is no good in these evils, but Jesus promises to work even atrocities together for his good. Our mighty God—for whom nothing is too difficult—*is* able to help you. I've had the privilege of working with women across the country who have endured horrors that could have made them bitter forever. These brave sisters have *chosen* to see and seek healing through forgiveness.

The people who have wronged you, and those who have wounded me, do not deserve to be forgiven. But neither do I . . . or you. We receive forgiveness *and* extend it only and ever because of grace, the undeserved gift of God through Jesus Christ. As hard as this is to accept, especially when those who have wounded us never acknowledge their wrong, we do not stand above those who have hurt us. We, like them, are debtors who can never repay our debts. When we know our place of approval and acceptance *in* Jesus, we can allow him to defend and avenge us, in his way and his time (see Rom. 12:19). You and I can decisively determine to leave the "other guy" to God and allow Jesus's goodness to work in us.

Through the power of redemption, forgiveness acts like spiritual surgery, not on the other person, but on your own soul. Forgiveness sets *you* free so that you can have friendships without bitterness, family relationships without resentment. Doesn't that sound good? I don't say this because it's easy, but because it's true: the choice is yours. Today "I have set before you life and death, blessings and curses. Now choose life, so that you and your children may live and that you may love the Lord your God, listen to his voice, and hold fast to him. For the Lord is your life" (Deut. 30:19–20).

If someone knocked on the door of your home and offered you life or death, blessings or curses, I'm guessing you would see the choice as a no-brainer. Unfortunately, decisions get terribly muddled when unforgiveness and bitterness enter the mix. All too often, we choose death and curses, in the form of resentment, rather than letting go and trusting God's ability to bring life and blessings out of circumstances that look only awful to us.

My friend, there is no plan B for life in Christ. Forgiveness is the plan, *the only plan*, for those "forever in" with Jesus (that's you!). Colossians 3:13 puts it plainly: "Remember, the Lord forgave you, so you *must* forgive others" (NLT, emphasis added). The glorious truth, laid out in 2 Corinthians 5:21, is this: you will never experience a wound at anyone's hands that Jesus didn't feel, bear, and overcome on Calvary. He took on *every sin* so that he could take all of them away. You are never alone in this fight!

Some people wrongly believe that forgiveness puts them in a position of vulnerability and weakness; it's no wonder these women default to bitterness! Nothing could be further from the biblical truth, however. Forgiveness only and ever flows from perfect strength, from a trust in the power of God to right wrongs, in the justice of his Son, and in the security of being forever "in." This acceptance is yours by right of adoption; the storehouse of heaven's joy and forgiveness is open to you, but you must enter through the Door, through Jesus. What do you have to lose but the bitterness that's poisoning you from the inside out?

You Can Bet . . .

I live in Southern California, where "brown" is advertised—I'm talking literally here—as "the new green" in drought-time lawn care. Perhaps that's why an anonymous quote I came across struck me so powerfully: "If the grass is greener on the other side of the fence, you can bet the water bill is higher."

Like bitterness, looking on the other side of the fence is a significant relationship destroyer. Trusting in our complete "in"ness helps us fight not only bitterness, but also envy and greed. Trusting that we're forever in with Jesus allows us to turn away from comparison and competition.

I find that envy and greed sneak up on Christian women like me. We don't wake up thinking, *Today I hope I'm terribly disappointed in everything I have and run into someone whose life looks perfectly together.* On the contrary, we often try to white-knuckle our way to contentment, ending up with lousy resignation instead.

Desperately striving to "stay satisfied" is not the path of life for a girl like you. Never forget that you are *already in.* And because you're in, you have a different set of choices available to you than to those on the outside. You no longer have to prove your worth by accumulating and accomplishing. As one of God's very own, you have been set free from the need to compare and compete. You, like Paul, can *learn* "the secret of being content in any and every situation, whether well fed or hungry, whether living in plenty or in want." Like you, "I can do all this through him who gives me strength" (Phil. 4:12–13). As Jesus asked Martha and Mary, I ask you: "Do you believe this?" (John 11:26). Do you really and truly believe this, to the point that your belief changes the way you think, act, and speak?

For those living on the "never enough" treadmills of comparison and competition, there's no rest or freedom. Being "in" with the "right" financial community, social circle, or elite crowd gives no lasting sense of peace. Of course these sorts of inner rings give people temporary pleasure and belonging. But they cannot—ever— give *life.* We must choose on which side of the door we will live. If we enter into eternal life in Jesus, "that means we will not compare ourselves with each other as if one of us were better and another worse. We have far more interesting things to do with our lives. Each of us is an original" (Gal. 5:25 MSG).

Six tiny words that alter everything: *Each of us is an original.*

According to Ephesians 2:10, you are an original masterpiece of God's design. Your life is a unique masterpiece that neither can—nor should!—be compared "as if one of us were better and another worse." Over years of wrestling with this, I have clung to the words of the inimitable G. K. Chesterton: "There are two ways to get enough. One is to continue to accumulate more and more. The other is to desire less."⁹

When I actively *choose* to desire less, I escape entrapment and enjoy freedom in my relationships; this is a choice you can make too. If we're confident that being "in" with Jesus secures our position, we can rejoice with those who have more and share freely with those in need because we lack nothing (Ps. 23:1).

On the other hand, those who perpetually strive for *more* and *better* do damage to their relationships, whether consciously or inadvertently. There are few people more tiresome than those for whom nothing's ever good enough. I'd venture a guess that you don't want to be that kind of woman. You're already *in*. What could stuff possibly add to that?

If you answered comfort and ease, you're right. Physical stuff can mitigate the difficulties of this world, and some women trade their position of eternal peace for that which this world offers. In doing so, they act like Esau, who sold his birthright for a pot of stew. This didn't work out so well for Esau (see Gen. 25–27), and I promise that no physical comfort you can grasp for yourself—no padded bank account, luxury home, nor the lust after any such thing—will provide more than that stew did for Esau. It nourished him for a moment, then impoverished him for life. This is precisely what envy and greed do to us. This is how they destroy our relationships.

That's why Jesus warned, "Beware, and be on your guard against every form of greed; for not *even* when one has an abundance does his life consist of his possessions" (Luke 12:15 NASB). Life is not measured by what we own; it's not measured by what we achieve. Life truly is measured by love, how well we receive it from God, and how well we offer it to others. *Life is about learning to love, not learning to get stuff done.*

If you want your relationships to grow, learn to be content; learn to love. Here's some good news to get you started: you're perfectly in with the Master Teacher, and he promises to guide you in the process. In Psalm 16:11, David proclaimed, "You make known to me the path of life; you will fill me with joy in your presence, with eternal pleasures at your right hand." In his presence are joy and pleasure, not privation and want. Once again, the choice is yours.

More than Chitchat and Coffee

Once assured of our acceptance in Jesus, freed from the burden of bitterness and the cage of comparison, we can enjoy meaningful relationships with others. Each and every day, we have perfect freedom to experience the delights of being "in" with Jesus and "out" amongst people. On occasion we'll find great joy; other times we'll be, for lack of a better phrase, chewed up and spit out. This will hurt, but through both joys and sorrows, we can conduct our relationships with the confidence of a chosen and beloved daughter who knows she's forever in.

Women with this assurance love others from a place of depth and authenticity; they get below the surface and bring blessing into the lives of those with whom they interact. The Bible describes this as "goodness and mercy" following the sheep of God's flock (Ps. 23:6 KJV).

To understand this, consider how shepherd and pastor Philip Keller poignantly describes the unique effects sheep can have on the land:

> Sheep can, under mismanagement, be the most destructive livestock. In short, they can ruin and ravage land almost beyond remedy. But in bold contrast they can, on the other hand, be the most beneficial of all livestock if properly managed. . . . In ancient literature, sheep

were referred to as "those of the golden hooves"—simply because they were regarded and esteemed so highly for their beneficial effect on the land. In my own experience as a sheep rancher I have, in just a few years, seen two derelict ranches restored to high productivity and usefulness. More than this, what before appeared as depressing eyesores became beautiful, parklike properties of immense worth. Where previously there had been only poverty and pathetic waste, there now followed flourishing fields and rich abundance. In other words, goodness and mercy had followed behind my flocks. They left behind them something worthwhile, productive, beautiful and beneficial to both themselves, others and me.[10]

The Bible makes explicitly clear that "we are the sheep of his pasture" (Ps. 100:3). Because of this, it's important that we ask ourselves: In my relationships with others,

- Do I leave behind peace or turmoil?
- Do I leave behind forgiveness or bitterness?
- Do I leave behind contentment or conflict?
- Do I leave behind joy or complaining?
- Do goodness and mercy follow me?

Knowing that you are eternally "in" enables you to leave marks of beauty and benefit on every single one of your relationships. Since you aren't trying to prove yourself—you're already fully "in"—you can love generously and graciously.

You can also see past the externals and into the heart of others. I like how Beth Moore articulates this: "That Prada bag on someone's shoulder may look impressive, but it still holds junk. Every person deals with secret pain."[11] Dear friend, how true I've found this to be! Indeed, it's more often than not the very woman with the impressive titles, "perfect" body, or expensive shoes who harbors the deepest secrets.

That was certainly the case for me many years back, when I covered the shame of an eating disorder and the fear that I'd never be loved if people "really knew me" with an artificially constructed, seemingly perfect exterior of pristine educational credentials, carefully coiffed appearance, and loads of Bible knowledge (little of which penetrated my hurting heart). I remember confessing my battle to a group of my peers and having people surround me afterward with comments like, "I never thought I could get close to you; you seemed to have everything. I'm so sorry that I didn't know you were hurting." I had taken the risk that being "in" with Jesus meant I could be "in" with his people, accepted just as I was. It was like water on my parched soul.

Many years ago, Scottish pastor John Watson reminded people to "be kind; everyone you meet is fighting a hard battle."[12] Isn't that *so* true?! How different would our world be if we all lived with this in mind?

I know I'm in with Jesus . . . 100 percent. I have nothing to prove and no one to prove it to. This frees me to be kind, to be gentle, to be loving, patient, and forgiving. I'm not claiming I always *choose* to be so—how terrible that there's evidence to support the opposite—but I am growing in this kind of friendship. I desire it in my marriage, in my parenting, as I relate to extended family, friends, colleagues, and even with customer service representatives from the IRS who have kept me on hold for forty-seven minutes while listening to canned Muzak (yes, even them).

My relationship with Jesus, being "in" with him, has made me richer in love and grace than I ever imagined I would be. I want to spend that wealth on people, loving them as Jesus has loved me. I invite you to the same. As women, let's get beyond chitchat and coffee. Let's stop gossiping and start loving more authentically. Let's make goodness and mercy the marks of our relationships, not comparison and competition. Let's exercise our perfect freedom in Jesus, freedom to forgive, to come in to sweet fellowship with him and go out to fulfilling friendship with others. I won't settle for anything less, and as one who has been invited eternally *in*, neither should you!

Practicing the Prayer of Examen

Even superanalytical women like me—who would love nothing more than to unplug my brain now and then—don't usually take stock of our daily lives. We may spin on and on about certain issues, worries, ideas, or dreams, but very few of us actually examine our day-to-day experiences. Doing so richly blesses your fellowship in Jesus, however, so I encourage you to try the ancient practice sometimes called "The Prayer of Examen."

While the prayer of examen can be done in many ways, I find the simplest way to start involves asking two questions at the close of the day:

- When did I feel closest to or most alive in Christ today?
- When did I feel farthest from him, most drained or discouraged?

The prayer of examen helps us determine patterns. It crystallizes times, circumstances, and/or relationships that draw you nearer to Jesus or drive you from him. As you begin to identify ways in which your life helps or hinders your fellowship with God and others, you can make changes accordingly.

For instance, some years ago, I noticed that I felt discouraged and depleted after shopping trips. I felt ugly, frumpy, and generally dissatisfied when I went to the mall, so I just stopped going. Of course I still had to buy clothes for the family, etc., but I did not have to frequent the mall, where messages of my "not enoughness" seemed to scream loudly from every storefront. Realizing that shopping depleted me meant identifying new ways to hang out with certain friends, but it was worth the effort. If I hadn't taken the time to observe this pattern in my life, I never would have experienced the freedom that comes from rejecting messages of comparison and competition (i.e., messages that make me feel "out") and making room for more time with the God who calls me forever "in."

On a positive note, I also recognized particular patterns in my relationships. I found that when I spent time with some friends, my outlook on life and my confidence in Christ soared. I purposed to be with them more, to thank God for them, and to express my gratitude to them for building me up. My friendships strengthened!

As you learn to practice it, the prayer of examen can be used over longer periods of time (e.g., weekly, monthly, and yearly). It can also help you pinpoint patterns at work, in marriage, or parenting. For example, if you want to use examen to edify your marriage, make the questions specific to your marital relationship: When has my marriage brought me closer to you over the last week, Lord? When has it taken me away from you? As always, the purpose is to allow the Holy Spirit to identify ways *you* can grow and change. Examen is *not* a time to review all of your spouse's, children's, co-workers', or friends' flaws; it is a time for you to observe and allow the Spirit to move in you.

This is a precious privilege of being forever *in* with Jesus; he loves us so much that he'll never let us stay in a place that's less than what he desires for us. God can use examen to help us recognize mistakes and wrong decisions; by his grace, Jesus then turns those into opportunities for our growth. May you and I be open to seeing what he wants us to see!

~~~~

Questions for Personal Reflection or Group Discussion

1. What kind of "inner rings" are Christian women attracted to? How does the lure of being "in" impact your life?
2. "Be kind; everyone you meet is fighting a hard battle." How might your life be different if you acted on this truth?
3. Practice examen and journal about or discuss your experience.

Recommended Reading

- Keller, Philip. *A Shepherd Looks at Psalm 23*. Grand Rapids: Zondervan, 1996.
- Smedes, Lewis. *The Art of Forgiving: When You Need to Forgive and Don't Know How*. New York: Ballantine Books, 1996; and *Forgive and Forget: Healing the Hurts We Don't Deserve*. New York: Harper San Francisco, 1997.

{5}

Satisfying Your True Hunger

There was once a man who planned a lavish feast for his entire community. The preparations were extensive: lovely invitations were issued, a succulent menu was planned, exquisite table decorations were handcrafted. Every carefully executed detail proclaimed the host's generosity and graciousness, for he genuinely loved his people.

As the time for the party drew near, the host looked out over a deserted ballroom. Sorrow filled his heart. Where was everyone?

Immediately he dispatched several assistants to contact the guests. Emails and texts flew into cyberspace, phones rang, and social media posts pleaded, "Please let us know if your plans have changed."

Responses came flooding in:

"I'm so sorry; I heard how decadent the food was going to be, and it will be much too tempting for me. I'm already struggling to keep my weight down!"

"I ended up having a really big lunch; I'm still so full! I couldn't possibly eat anything right now."

"You probably haven't even considered my intolerances! At the last banquet, all I could eat were a few asparagus stalks. I'll just stay home."

"I haven't made it to the gym today; I won't be coming after all."

What pitiful excuses the host had to endure, each one more flimsy and hurtful than the last! He directed the assistants: "Go into the streets. Round up anyone who's hungry, anyone who will feast with me. I planned this dinner to be savored, and I will enjoy it with anyone who comes."

Those who stayed home continued their calculated and controlled lives while those who came were blessed by the host's liberality and love. They were the ones who lived happily ever after.

~~~~~

As some of you may have recognized, this little story modernizes Jesus's "Parable of the Great Feast" from Luke 14:12–24. As I prepared to write about the enmity between women, their bodies, and food, it struck me that for many years, I would have been counted among the "excuse-makers" in Jesus's tale. Over the course of my forty-plus years, I've ranged from being obsessed with eating the "right" foods to consistently overindulging, to dieting and exercising in stringent ways. I've cut carbs and curtailed other food groups, cleansed and purified. Basically, I've tried it all, so when I came across the following words, they stuck like a thorn in my "carbs lead to fat" thinking:

> Then Jesus declared, "I am the bread of life. Whoever comes to me will never go hungry, and whoever believes in me will never be thirsty. But as I told you, you have seen me and still you do not believe." (John 6:35–36)

All women have a primal need for nourishment; at the same time, most have deeply conflicted relationships with their bodies and food. In John 6, Jesus invites us to the freedom of living a genuinely satisfied life. The question is, *Do we have an appetite for it?*

The When, Where, and Why

John chapter 5 records a beautiful moment in Jesus's ministry. From one boy's lunch, broken with thanksgiving, thousands are not only fed; they *feast*. The flabbergasted disciples collect twelve baskets of leftovers. It's all so lavish and lovely. What would it have been like to be there?

Apparently it didn't impact the people of Jesus's day in the same way I picture it transforming me. One would think those following Christ would say, "He has power to provide and does it generously; *this* is someone we can trust!" Instead, they chase Jesus down and ask him to put miracle food on auto-pay: "Give us that bread every day of our lives."[1] Jesus's followers wanted manna—daily provision, like their ancestors had eaten while wandering in the wilderness with Moses.

Jesus responds, "Don't you understand? Moses was simply the delivery boy—the bread came from God himself. And now, our Father is offering you the bread of life, for *I AM* the bread of life. Feed on me, and you'll never again ache with hunger deep inside; nor will your spirit thirst anymore. You go on and on about Moses and his bread from the skies—but your ancestors still died! *I AM* life-giving bread. Eat this bread and you'll live forever. This life-giving bread is my body. When it is broken, it will offer the whole world a chance at life everlasting."[2]

I find it fascinating and horrifying that the crowd is less than a day removed from a miracle of epic proportions, yet they're back to asking, "What can you do for us now, Jesus?" They're hungry again and they prefer being full. Honestly, who doesn't? The problem with chasing fullness, however, is that if we're not feeding on the right things, nothing's ever quite *enough*. More often than not, hunger makes us consumers rather than enjoyers.[3]

God wrote into the universe a specific plan: through eating we would sustain physical life. He designed food to be taken in, converted into energy by our marvelously designed bodies, then released into our cells, giving us vitality and strength.

In a similar manner, through spiritual nourishment, God created the life of the soul to be sustained. Apart from Christ, every woman is famished by sin. I have felt the starvation of living my own agenda, and I suspect you've sensed it too, even if you didn't realize what it was. When we choose to receive Jesus as the Bread of Life, however, vigor returns to our spirits, vivacity to our hearts and minds. And the good news doesn't stop here: while physical food is broken down and absorbed, leaving us hungry later, the very opposite is true of spiritual nourishment. Jesus imparts life continuously; the Bread of Life is never expended.

Biologically speaking, hunger reminds us to eat. Without food and water, we perish, so hunger pangs are a gift of mercy from God to a people who forget to do what's best for them, who get tricked into thinking they can satisfy their needs elsewhere, or who dismiss their emptiness with various denial techniques (keeping busy or trying to maintain control have been my go-to distractions). We can only disregard or malnourish our bodies for so long, however. The same applies to our spirits.

Women suffer from a deeper hunger than we often recognize, a hunger of the heart that can only be satisfied with the Bread of Life—God himself. Sadly, most of us pay attention to this hunger only when things get desperate. We run to God when nothing else seems to work. We spend time, money, and energy trying to fill ourselves with substitutes that don't last and can never give real *life*. For many women, this includes a fixation on food and body image. Whether women overeat junk or carefully select every calorie for its nutrient power, whether they exercise obsessively or verbally abuse their bodies again and again, this is an all-too-common battle.

And, really, that shouldn't shock us. Scottish pastor Iain Campbell shrewdly notes, "It was through eating that we lost communion with God: Adam ate forbidden food and all mankind fell into sin. And it is also by eating the bread of God's providing that life and vitality are restored to our souls. If we do not eat, we die in our sins."[4] Eating plays a powerful role in the life of faith! Indeed, we are called to feed on God daily through his Word: "I have treasured the words of his mouth more than my daily bread," proclaimed Job (23:12).

I'll be blunt with you: a lot of days I've "treasured my daily bread" (or exercise or chocolate) a lot more than God's words. Have you ever been tempted to spend your life on things that don't ultimately satisfy?

That's Why He Chose Bread

In order to write this chapter, I spent a lot of time reading commentaries on John 6. Without exception, each book articulated something along these lines: bread is a "staple of every cultural diet," "foundational to every meal," "something that everyone needs and likes." I found it somewhat odd reading these statements as a twenty-first-century girl in Southern California, where bread has an extremely bad reputation.

A *lot* of women I know adamantly refuse bread rather than gladly receive it. Whether they do so because they're severely allergic, have chosen a gluten-free or low-carb lifestyle, believe bread is a source of poor nutrition, or for some other reason, these gals look down on bread rather than see it as a "staple" or "foundation" of their daily meals. Some women I know aren't able to (those with celiac disease) or simply choose not to take communion at their churches because there's no gluten-free option available. For many years I was so concerned about my carb intake that I would look for the smallest possible piece of communion bread and the scantiest cupful of juice. How sad I feel for that younger me; how starving I now see she was for true fulfillment!

This is, of course, not descriptive of every woman. I have plenty of friends with whom I can now relish the "Hot bread!" call our local bakery-café workers shout when baguettes are fresh out of the oven. Enjoying bread like this is much more in line with what Jesus's followers would have experienced. They saw bread as fundamentally important for life; it was essential, and beyond that, it was *good*.

It's a fascinating dynamic for me, as a teacher of God's Word, to have to convince women that the Bread of Life is a beautiful and life-giving image, not one that will lead to excess weight, bloating, or some other form of discomfort. If you ask me, the enemy's hand is evident here; of course he'd want to destroy the very pictures God used to describe himself!

Take a moment and imagine yourself as a woman hearing Jesus say—for the first time—"*I am* the bread of life. If you feed on me, you won't go hungry again." Try to sense what it would've been like to hear this invitation: "Come! With me you won't ever feel the ache of hunger again." Doesn't some part of that sound so freeing, so right, so true?

No one comes to Jesus and discovers that the nourishment he gives produces an allergic reaction. No one feeds on the words of Scripture and feels distended. No one needs a special enzyme to digest the Bread of Life. And what joy: the food he provides our spirit is not only nutritious; it's delicious too!

The psalmist urged people to "taste and see that the Lord is good" because he *is* good (Ps. 34:8). You will not find him wanting. Everything else is like boiled turnips and beet juice compared to the delight of feasting with Jesus. And while Mountain Dew and Twinkies may taste good on the way down, we know what junk food ultimately does to our bodies. God's nourishment is sweet *and* satisfying; it lacks neither taste nor sustenance. There's no "a moment on the lips, a lifetime on the hips" quandary here.

I adore how Psalm 36 describes the satisfaction God's people enjoy: "How priceless is your unfailing love, O God! People take refuge in the shadow of your wings. They feast on the abundance of your house; you give them drink from your river of delights. For with you is the fountain of life; in your light we see light" (vv. 7–9). God is not trying to stuff poached chicken, wilted broccoli, and a wafer-thin slice of sprouted-grain toast down your throat. Jesus invites us to *feast on the abundance of his house*. He offers us generous and lavish love.

We cannot, however, stand outside the door and simply admire the feast. No sustenance comes from being an expert on nutrition (physical or spiritual). No one can eat bread for you, nor can they force you to eat. Learning to make bread may satisfy the hunger inside you for creativity and activity, but you must *eat* physically and take in the Bread of Life spiritually if you are to be truly fulfilled.

Because of Jesus, you and I don't have to forage on our own anymore; we can feast whenever we like! Though it cost God a great deal—the excruciating execution of and complete alienation from his Son—the Bread of Life is free to you and me. Heaven's bread was purchased at the highest price so it might be offered to you at no price at all. That, my friend, is very good news.

Where to Get Food That Is Good for the Soul

I struggled for years detesting my body, treating it wretchedly, alternatively fearing food or fixating on it, generally obsessing about my weight, appearance, what I put in my mouth, and when. It's a horrid way to live, and I am eternally grateful God set me free from that. I really do understand when my sisters in Christ describe the challenges of developing and maintaining positive body image and a balanced approach to eating. Some of you are internally scoffing now: Is that even possible?!

Statistics don't present a pretty picture in response. A recent nationwide survey revealed that 97 percent of women have a minimum of one cruel body thought a day. Lest you limit this to those who "feel fat," let me assure you that even thin girls struggle with their appearance. Whether they hate their bony legs, fight problem skin, or wish they filled bigger bra cups, your friends who don't battle "the bulge" may feel as insecure—or more so—than those who lament their muffin tops. Researchers determined that the average woman entertains thirteen negative judgments each day about her weight, appearance, or physical body; that's a stinging thought for each waking hour. Some confessed having fifty, one hundred, or more every day.[5] You know what I think about the other 3 percent? They're lying.

Okay, maybe not, but I honestly wonder how those women get through a day without feeling "less than" when looking at the magazines in a checkout line, the billboards for fast-food restaurants featuring models who've clearly never eaten a bacon cheeseburger in their lives, and TV shows with nipped, tucked, enhanced, and carefully selected women from the top tier of beauty. Of course there are the token character actresses who've been chosen for things other than their physical appearance, but who among us wants to be in that camp? Yeah, I thought so.

It was horrifying, though not entirely shocking, for me to read the results of another survey, which found that 16 percent of young women would trade a year of life for their ideal body weight and shape. Ten percent were willing to trade two to five years, and 2 percent were willing to trade up to ten years of life away. One percent said they would give up twenty-one years or more. I'm not making this up![6]

Before jumping to conclusions about these gals, I had to authentically evaluate what I'd be willing to give up to have a "perfect" body and face. Would I give up a year of my life? God, have mercy on me. There have been times I might have seen that as a good idea.

Some years ago, I began rereading the Bible in a new-to-me translation. I spent so many years memorizing from and reading in the NASB and NIV translations that I realized my brain was mindlessly scanning the page but not engaging with the truth. A mentor recommended I try reading from another translation, so I started using one of my husband's old Bibles, not thinking it would make that much difference. Oh, how very wrong I was! Passages I'd read many times began to dance off the page and into my heart. I was captivated once again with how living and active God's Word genuinely is.

One such portion of Scripture was Isaiah 55. As a woman who understood far better the thirteen-cruel-body-thoughts-a-day group than the 3 percent who looked at food and their figures with balance, God's truth fell on me like warm summer rain:

> Is anyone thirsty? Come and drink—even if you have no money! Come, take your choice of wine or milk—it's all free! Why spend your money on food that does not give you strength? Why pay for food that does you no good? Listen, and I will tell you where to get food that is good for the soul! Come to me with your ears wide open. Listen, for the life of your soul is at stake. (Isaiah 55:1–3 NLT 1996)

It may strike you as strange, but I literally wept at the idea that I'd chased "food" that gave me no strength for so long, that I'd paid heavily for "food" that did me no good. I knew that the life of my soul was at stake and that, like it or not, the way I viewed my body was a big part of the battle for the health of my spirit.

Dallas Willard once observed that, for better or for worse, the body lies at the very center of a God-honoring life.[7] We may not talk about this at church all that often, but I believe most women sense, even if we're not keen to recognize it, that body image (and the way we feel about ourselves as a result of our body image) forms a major roadblock to joy and peace in our relationship with God.

God's Word doesn't shy away from talking about the spiritual implications of our physical choices. Indeed, the Bible clearly commands, "So whether you eat or drink or whatever you do, do it all for the glory of God" (1 Cor. 10:31) and "Do not tear down the work of God for the sake of food" (Rom. 14:20 NASB). The book of Philippians decries those whose "god is their stomach" (3:19), and Paul explicitly compares the body to God's holy temple, a place of beauty and splendor, goodness and glory, *not* something to be insulted and abused (1 Cor. 6:19).

We spend money—and loads of it—on not only material food, which we may waver between using for comfort or control, but also on "food" of other kinds, things we think will make life better: diet aids or wrinkle creams, gym memberships or fashionable fitness wear. Some research estimates that urban women spend a full third of their income on appearance-modifying products and services, and they consider this a *necessary* investment.[8] Beyond money, we spend insane amounts of time and energy on what does not satisfy. You may be able to buy tighter pores, but you can't hide forever from the truth of aging; you may be able to maintain taut muscles, but you can't avoid your own vulnerability. You can buy bigger boobs, a flatter stomach, or a pixie nose, but having these won't heal the ache inside to be loved and accepted.

Jesus never said to stop caring for the needs of the body. Treating his temple well is wise and important. That said, God does put his finger on a deep heart issue common to women: excessive attention to temporary things can lead to neglect of the soul. In his tremendous mercy, Jesus invites us to a better way. Tragically, too many women respond, "I'm full." "I've got my sweat to get on." "I've got my intolerances to control, my skin-care regime to stick to, my needs to meet." "*Thanks anyway.*"

According to John 6, the vast majority of the crowd who listened to Jesus proclaim himself "the Bread of Life" walked away, returning to a life spent on "what does not satisfy" (Isa. 55:2). Perhaps you're quick to explain, "But that's not me; I may struggle with negative body thoughts, but it doesn't mean I've rejected Jesus."

Of course not! Your salvation doesn't depend on whether you have a positive body image. The vitality of your soul may, however.

Dear one, don't be fooled; everyone labors for some kind of "food." If you're not actively choosing to eat the Bread of Life, you're feeding on something else. Maybe you're feeding on the control of healthy eating—you're careful and proud of it. You don't spend a third of your income on beauty products, but perhaps you do on supplements or naturopathic products. Perhaps you're feeding on the dreams of a beach body or just one Saturday when you didn't blow your diet. Maybe you're so careless with your food choices that you're feeding on junk and thinking this is a better way than those vain women who are so obsessed with their bodies. I'm not judging your choices; I'm asking you to consider, with the Holy Spirit's guidance and grace, what are you *truly* feeding on?

I attend a church that celebrates communion in a specifically Protestant way. Sometimes, however, I visit my parents' congregation and participate in the liturgy of the Eucharist. When I do, I treasure the words spoken over me as I receive the bread: "Take and eat this in remembrance that Christ died for you, and feed on him in your heart."[9]

Are you feeding on Christ's words about you in faith and with thanksgiving? Are you grateful for your body? Can you savor food with joy, as a gift from God? Can you speak about and treat your body with dignity, respect, and delight? If you can't, do you even see that as a problem? Christ chose a *meal* as the means of remembering him, and the image of *bread* to proclaim the truth of his character. The enemy wants to set your mind against food and your own body because he knows that doing so leaves you famished in both body and spirit.

In order to find food that is good for the soul, in order to develop an appetite for the Bread of Life, I believe women must fight for their freedom from the tyranny of food and weight control, negative body thoughts, and the fear of growing old. By engaging in this battle, we labor for peace of mind and loving liberty. This is food that gives strength and satisfaction. I'd like to close this chapter with some specific suggestions for choosing freedom and experiencing Jesus's sustenance daily.

So What Can I Do?

Take the two-week challenge. Most women have no idea how often they speak damaging words over themselves. They mindlessly chatter about "hating" their thighs or bellies, "regretting" what they ate, vowing to "do better" or "try harder." It's time we join together to stop this nonsense!

I invite you to fast for two weeks from verbalizing negative self-talk. That's right, no "I'm never going to fit in my pants tomorrow," "I feel so fugly" (translation: fat + ugly), "I hate my _____," "I shouldn't have eaten that" comments for two whole weeks. Try it. Seriously, what have you got to lose?

Important note: I'm not asking you to control the thoughts that fly unbidden into your head—especially if you've allowed this area of your thought life to go unattended for some time; instead, I'm asking you to decide what comes out of your mouth. During these two weeks, you may find that an intense battle in your mind reveals itself. That's okay. Start with a deliberate choice to refrain from aligning your spoken words with the destructive thoughts in your mind. Some of these ideas are merely the result of habit (perhaps you've thought poorly about yourself for so long that your mind is festering with cruel self-judgments); others are negative ideas introduced by the world, the enemy, and those around you (fasting from any guilt-inducing relationships during this time may also be in order).

I promise you, the freedom that you will experience if you actually devote yourself to this two-week challenge will spur you on to greater conviction that laboring for that which gives life—and make no mistake, this will feel like *hard work* for some of us—is worth every effort.

Find better things to do. In Galatians 5:25–26 Paul proclaims, "Let us not become conceited, provoking and envying each other." Another translation renders Paul's words: "We have far more interesting things to do with our lives. Each of us is an original" (MSG).

Do you have better things to do with your life than evaluate your body and diet? What about the fitness, attractiveness, and food choices of your friends, family members, and celebrities? Hmm . . . It would be hard to justify a negative response: "Nope. I've got nothing better to do."

Perhaps we should start with, "Do you *want* to let go of comparison and competition?" If so, find better things to do.

There's absolutely nothing wrong—in fact there are so many beautiful things right—with taking care of the masterpiece that God created in your body. I certainly feel better when I eat well and exercise appropriately. I *never, ever* feel better about myself when I glance at swimsuit-edition magazines while I'm checking out at the store, read about how fast so-and-so lost her pregnancy fat, or the ways she stays "hot" at fifty years old. It has never, ever strengthened or satisfied me to sit in church, distracted and distressed because I feel less attractive than that new woman I saw in the courtyard. I have better things to do. So do you.

Some of those better things may involve ways to treat your body well. I encourage you to do that! But do it because they *give you strength*, not because you think they'll alter your appearance. Don't labor for that which is not bread—circumstantial change—when what gives life is feeding on truth, goodness, and beauty.

Allow me to gently suggest one "better thing" in which you can invest energy and time: your spiritual growth. I both appreciated and was convicted by the words of a pastor I respect deeply. I'd like to share his challenging questions with you: "Are you too easily satisfied? Are you growing in your faith? Do you care if you're not? . . . Does your relationship with God really shape the way you think about and act in your marriage, in your friendships, in your parenting, in your job, in your finances . . . or in your secret thoughts and desires? As you examine yourself, are you able to be satisfied in places where God is not?"[10]

Hebrews 5:14 tells us that mature believers have powers of discernment trained *by constant practice.* In other words, it takes time and effort to grow. Complacency and apathy happen naturally; spiritual growth does not. If you spend your energy on aligning yourself with God's truth, feeding on the Bread of Life, you'll find that you can readily distinguish between good and bad, better and best in your own life, and that is something *far better* to do than comparing and competing with those around you.

Evaluate to what and where you run. Bottom line, we return to things that give us a sense of fulfillment, even if it's only momentary. That's the basis not only of positive experiences like going back to our favorite restaurants, but also damaging ones like substance abuse, emotionally dysfunctional relationships, obsession with health and fitness, or other distractions from the abundant life Jesus offers.

Take stock of the patterns of your life. You may be surprised. Most of us are so busy (and consequently exhausted), that we don't actually realize we run to some dismal places and things when we're hurting, tired, or upset. Whether it's a screen or a fridge, a treadmill or a relationship, start taking an inventory of the things, places, and people to which you run.

Please don't let yourself off the hook by reading this and letting it go past both eyes and out your brain. Stop right now, find a piece of paper, and ask the Holy Spirit, "Please show me at least one thing I run to for fullness instead of you." I believe he will faithfully reveal things to you if you ask and listen. It's okay to start small. You can always ask him to show you more later. Consider sharing what you hear with a trusted friend, mentor, or accountability partner. Choose to obey whatever it is the Holy Spirit asks you to do instead of running to another thing, person, or feeling. Life is yours for the choosing; feed on that which gives you strength.

Ruthlessly eliminate busyness from your life. Frantic, stressed-out living leads to poor choices with food and the body. I seriously doubt any reader would deny this, yet most of us persist on a life treadmill that eventually throws us off-kilter. Bottom line, "Either hunger for God is the sun around which I organize everything, or else God is just one object among others orbiting the very crowded sky of my life."[11] When you have space in your life, margin that allows you to evaluate choices and make better ones, you grow spiritually and can learn to treat your body as God designed. We'll have occasion to discuss the practice of rest and margin later in the book, so keep your eyes open while you determine now to begin ruthlessly eliminating busyness from your life.

Don't take the edge off. Many women lead very full, but none-theless dissatisfied lives. There is a striking difference between being full and being content. Many of us are full of noise, communication, stuff, options, and opportunities, but being driven by this kind of fullness doesn't lead to serenity. As a result, we take the edge off uncomfortable emotions with activities like shopping, work, even "perfect parenting" or service at church. Others numb painful emotions with a glass or taste of something calming and savory.

One way to find peace with your body and food is to press into uncomfortable emotions rather than dismiss or run away from them. God tells us, "Blessed are those who mourn, for they will be comforted" (Matt. 5:4). It's rather tough to accept, but this verse makes clear that we have to go through the pain in order to receive the comfort. Don't try to avoid the shame, fear, anger, disappointment, or _____ (you fill in the blank) that may drive you to think about and treat your body poorly. Press into the pain because that's where you'll find Jesus.

When you originally said yes to him, you gave up the right to do with your body whatever you choose. Maybe you didn't catch that in the spiritual fine print, but I promise you, he asks you to surrender for your own good. It is for *freedom* that Christ has set you free (Gal. 5:1). Isn't that wonderful? He wants to liberate you from the painful emotions that you try to numb. As you come more and more under his gracious control, you'll find that you see yourself differently—with the loving eyes through which he sees you—and treat yourself accordingly. When you feed on the Bread of Life, you don't have to force a healthy body image or relationship with food. Being close to him brings the fruit of self-control, peace, gentleness, and love organically.

Align yourself with truth. It's absolutely essential that you don't simply let go of lies like "If I look a certain way or weigh a certain amount, I'll feel 'good enough,'" "If I can't have everything, at least I can look good," "Thin equals beautiful," or "When life is out of control, at least I can decide what I will and won't eat." You must actively replace faulty thinking with God's truth and act differently as a result. Remember, it's your thoughts that determine the course of your life. Your behavior and habits spring from your thoughts, so when the voice of accusation shouts, "You shouldn't have eaten that. What are you doing? Do you want to be fat?" or "No one will ever love you if you look like that," make sure you're armed with God's truth.

Our culture operates on an intricate and insidious "thin myth," in which a slender body represents not only attractiveness but also self-sacrifice, virtue, success, and control."[12] Our culture also sends the message that there are some "good" and some "bad" body types. I encourage you to expose any and every lie you've heard or believed to the light of God's truth. Develop the habit of treating your body with respect and honor, the way God treats you. Speaking his word out loud may help; it's certainly helped me! Next time a negative body thought comes, choose one of the following: "I am God's masterpiece, created in Christ Jesus for good works" (see Eph. 2:10); "I will not tear down the work of God for the sake of food or the myth of a perfect body" (see Rom. 14:20); "My god is not my stomach or my thighs or any other part of my body" (see Phil. 3:19); or "I am part of God's beauty and splendor here on earth, a temple for him" (see 1 Cor. 6:19). At first, this practice may feel strange. That's okay. Do it anyway because truth sets you free (John 8:32) and these are truths regardless of whether you *feel* them or not.

Practicing the Prayer of Contentment (a.k.a. Sleeping with Bread)

World War II left thousands homeless and helpless. Allied troops and European natives placed orphaned children in refugee camps or group homes where they could receive medical attention, proper nutrition, and education. Despite the fact that they were safe and even lovingly cared for, however, many of the children couldn't sleep at night. Every effort was expended to help, all to no avail.

Finally, one of the supervising psychologists put forward a rather odd idea: Let's send the children to bed each night with a piece of bread. If they want more to eat, we'll provide it, but this slice is simply for them to hold.

To the great astonishment of the caretakers, the situation dramatically altered. With bread in their hands, the children slept peacefully and awoke with greater confidence and less anxiety. Simply knowing that provision was available, that they would eat tomorrow, even if only this one slice of bread, allowed the children to rest. They could worry about one less thing.[13]

I invite you to sleep tonight—and *every* night—being held by the Bread of Life. You don't even have to hold on to him; he does the holding!

Here's how you do it: As you lie down to sleep, ask Jesus to be your peace. Deliberately surrender any negative thoughts about yourself, your body, or food. Tell him you want to be satisfied by his provision and thank him for what he's given. Practice this simple prayer of contentment and tell people you sleep with bread. At the very least you'll get some interesting responses.

Questions for Personal Reflection or Group Discussion

1. Is it easy or difficult to see yourself as God's masterpiece? Why?

2. Are you willing to take the two-week challenge? Why or why not? What do you think you might experience?

3. Journal about or discuss the following: "There is a striking difference between being full and being content. Many of us are full of noise, communication, stuff, options, and opportunities, but being driven by this kind of fullness doesn't lead to serenity." In what ways are you tempted to "take the edge off" in your life? Jesus wants to set you free from painful emotions you try to numb. Will you let him? Talk with him about it in prayer.

Recommended Reading

- Rhodes, Constance. *Life Inside the Thin Cage*. Colorado Springs: Shaw Books, 2010. Constance founded a wonderful ministry called Finding Balance. Help and hope are available for you at ww.findingbalance.org.

- Strickland, Jennifer. *Girl Perfect*. Lake Mary, FL: Excel Books, 2008.

{6}

I'm Not Afraid of the Dark Anymore

If you're afraid of creepy-crawly things, you may want to skip the following section. Fairly warned? Okay, my brave remaining readers, let me recount to you the harrowing tale of my husband's summer in Reseda, California.

At the virtual center of the Los Angeles Basin, Reseda is a concrete jungle where summer sun causes sidewalks to sizzle with shimmering heat. It was somewhere near a zillion degrees when my husband, Jeramy, pulled up to his boss's house. Derek had offered Jeramy a place to stay while he interned for the summer: "I've got a couch in my garage; you can totally crash there."

Perhaps Jeramy imagined a little more than exposed two-by-fours and a threadbare sofa. Maybe Derek unrolling a spare rug and watching a cloud of dust plume from it like the fallout of an atom bomb distressed my sweetheart a tad. Still, nothing could have prepared Jeramy for what happened as he lay down to sleep that night.

In the inky darkness of Derek's garage, the scritch-scratch of tiny feet startled my husband from half sleep. Flicking on the light, Jeramy scanned the garage floor but saw nothing. Unsatisfied with the evidence his eyes provided, he decided to move a box to investigate.

As Jeramy lifted the cardboard cube, time momentarily froze. Thirty pairs of beady bug eyes stared up at him. Antennae circled hypnotically above armor-plated black heads. In an instant, everything clicked back to life and the cockroaches scattered with lightning speed.

Trying unsuccessfully to ignore the abrasive sound of roach feet on concrete, Jeramy abandoned the garage and slept on Derek's living room couch for the night. But in his heart, a war had begun, a battle waged between man and bug from the dawn of time (or so I imagine).

The next day, Jeramy bought ammunition: roach motels and a poisonous powder, which he laid out in a thick white strip where garage and driveway met.

For some days, Jeramy came home to find cockroaches in various stages of demise. Those stuck in the roach motels were destined to a slow death by starvation. Those who crossed the white line expired quickly, as poison flooded their wicked little bug bloodstreams. (Has it become clear how much I detest roaches?!) Jeramy actually found tiny white footprints leading away from the line of doom. Those cockroaches never stood a chance (insert maniacal laugh here).

I wish you could hear my husband tell this story; he does it with such amazing sound and visual effects. I wish even more that this story had absolutely no connection to my life, but it does, at least metaphorically. This tale describes vividly how sin scurries into my mind and heart when I'm in the dark. Light exposes what's creeping and crawling inside of me, and—all too often—the first reaction of my sin nature is to scatter and hide from the light.

Instead of closing my eyes to the scritch-scratch of sin within me, I want to wage war. I want to live in the light, for God has called me out of darkness and into his marvelous light (1 Pet. 2:9). This is his call on your heart too. But God is not merely content to dole out light as a quantity to be used up, nor will he stand to be "a" light among others. Jesus proclaims,

> I am the light of the world. Whoever follows me will never walk in darkness, but will have the light of life. (John 8:12)

God, the Great I AM, is the universal Light to everyone, of everything. Apart from him, there is no light, for even the sun takes its cues from the Light of the World.

If I am to embrace Jesus and know who I am in him, I must courageously acknowledge and fight sin within me. The same is true for you. Sin keeps us from the light of life. It destroys our ability to see, blinding us to the truth. It keeps us stuck in pits of despair or disobedience. It deceives, drives doubt deep within, deforms our desires, divides us from love and freedom, and distracts us from the abundant life Christ died to give us.

Fortunately, though sin wields these powers, we can forever "thank God! He gives us victory over sin and death through our Lord Jesus Christ" (1 Cor. 15:57 NLT). We are not alone in the war against sin; the battle is the Lord's, and he fights fiercely on our behalf. My end is secure, and so is yours. We *never again* have to walk in darkness; the light of life is ours for all eternity.

The When, Where, and Why

Traditionally, the Hebrew people celebrated a number of feasts throughout the year; each had a specific purpose as well as a set of accompanying practices, clearly ordained by God. In the seventh month of the Jewish calendar, Yahweh commanded his people to observe the Festival of Tabernacles. It was a time of joyful thanksgiving for the harvest and also a time to remember their ancestors' exodus from slavery and forty years of desert wandering. During this festival, God directed the Hebrews to present special offerings, celebrate his faithful provision, rest from their work, and "live in temporary shelters for seven days. All native-born Israelites are to live in such shelters so your descendants will know that I had the Israelites live in temporary shelters when I brought them out of Egypt. I am the Lord your God" (Lev. 23:42–43).

When Jesus walked on earth, tradition dictated that four great lamps were lit in the temple each evening during the Festival of Tabernacles, commemorating the pillars of cloud and fire that accompanied the Israelites on their journey out of Egypt and into the Promised Land (see Exod. 13:21–22).

As the temple courtyards blazed with lights, the Hebrew people were reminded that God had faithfully provided food in the desert, faithfully protected them with shelter, and faithfully guided them. At the close of the feast, one lamp was traditionally left unlit, symbolizing the Jewish people's belief that true deliverance was still to come. God would provide a greater light, their Messiah, to deliver them from oppression and lead them into everlasting life. Indeed, based on the words of Daniel 2:22 and Psalm 27:1, Jewish scholars believed one of the Messiah's names would be "the Light."

On *this* stage, during a festival celebrating God's faithfulness and awaiting the provision of his Messiah, to a people expecting the Light to come, perhaps in the very temple courts where a single lamp stood unlit . . . *this* is when, where, and why Jesus proclaimed, "I am the light of the world" (John 8:12).

It could mean nothing less to the people of Israel than this: "*I am* the One you've been waiting for. Your Deliverer has come!" As the Feast of Tabernacles ended, Jesus wanted his people not merely to look back and remember what he'd done in the past; he longed for them to know his faithfulness and provision in the present tense.

Christ's words also imply that the world needs light. Darkness is the world's natural condition, and this is no small matter. Two thousand–plus amazing years of scientific progress, artistic expression, and philosophical pondering notwithstanding, the words of Isaiah 60:2 ring true: "Darkness covers the earth and thick darkness is over the peoples." The KJV uses the phrase "gross darkness," which I believe says it well for this day and age. Apart from the Light of the World, a sickeningly deep darkness covers the earth and its inhabitants, regardless of how enlightened people foolishly believe themselves to be without God.

Jesus came to dispel darkness, to be light and life to me, to guide me and help me. I don't have to be afraid of the dark anymore. It's ugly and sad to concede, but more often than not, when left to my own devices, I sink into the suffocating smallness of a darkened mind and heart. In Jesus's light, however, I see light (Ps. 36:9).

John's Gospel makes this explicit: "In him was life, and that life was the light of all mankind. The light shines in the darkness, and the darkness has not overcome it" (John 1:4–5).

The darkness has not overcome it. How we can praise God for this! But let me tell you, it ain't for darkness's lack of trying. The battle between light and darkness rages on, and the war is not fought merely on the battlegrounds of government buildings, courtrooms, or schools. The war is also inside of you, just as it is inside of me.

As people mired in a dark world, we desperately need light. We need light *inside* us, for the darkness within us is drawn to darkness around us. Sin is a darkness that starts within; you and I sin because parts of our hearts are still dark. That's why it's so important that we courageously and candidly look at the darkness inside. As we allow the Light of the World to shine his healing upon us, we "will never walk in darkness, but will have the light of life" (John 8:12).

Light Is as Light Does

I absolutely love that when Jesus comes on the scene, light becomes available to all. No one is excluded! Matthew 4:16 reveals, "The people living in darkness have seen a great light; on those living in the land of the shadow of death a light has dawned." With the incarnation, God makes darkness a choice. Because he freely offers light to all, one must *choose* to remain in the dark. Jesus affirms, "If you follow me, you won't *have* to walk in darkness, because you will have the light that leads to life" (John 8:12 NLT, emphasis added).

If we are to have this light, I believe we must recognize its properties and its effects. To know the Light is to receive and love him, to be filled with him, to reject darkness. Just as Jesus used the physical properties of bread to help us understand our need for nourishment and to overcome the enmity with our bodies, I believe he carefully chose the image of light to help us comprehend the darkness that threatens and the power his grace gives us.

Though the physical properties of light are manifold, I'd like to focus on a few: Light makes things visible; light reveals and exposes; it heals and transforms. Light provides heat, power, and guidance.

Light affects both seer and seen. It makes colors visible and stimulates the mind with what it illuminates. As the Light of the World, Jesus dramatically alters what we see and how we see it. C. S. Lewis famously observed, "I believe in Christianity as I believe that the sun has risen: not only because I see it, but because by it I see everything else."[1]

By Christ's light I see everything, and the more I allow his light to illuminate my mind and heart, the more I see the world for what it is: "groaning" and "suffering" to be "liberated from its bondage to decay and brought into the freedom and glory of the children of God" (see Rom. 8:21–23). Without Christ's light, things get muddled in my mind. A little bit of bad may not seem *that* bad anymore, and darkness creeps in. When the Light of Truth bursts into our lives, he changes how and what we see.

Light also scatters darkness; it has a penetrating, expelling, discerning quality to it. As we progress through this chapter, don't despair if areas of your life start to look a lot messier than you imagined. Moving toward light does that. Physical light dispels darkness, naturally creating separation; allowing the Light of the World access to your heart does too.

The same is true for light's propensity to expose. Spiritual light reveals things, particularly hidden, forgotten, or ignored things. Daniel 2:22 affirms, "He reveals deep and hidden things; he knows what lies in darkness, and light dwells with him." To most people, this sounds rather intimidating. And it should! As it shines on areas we've long avoided, light pierces disconcertingly. The Light of the World cannot allow us to remain comfortable in sin. His exposure of our sin may be painful at first, but our good and his glorious love lie on the other side.

Read the words of Ephesians 5:8–11, 13 carefully:

> For you were once darkness, but now you are light in the Lord. Live as children of light (for the fruit of the light consists in all goodness, righteousness and truth) and find out what pleases the Lord. Have nothing to do with the fruitless deeds of darkness, but rather expose them. . . . Everything exposed by the light becomes visible—and everything that is illuminated becomes a light.

Do you see the progression here? As you lean into exposure, everything illuminated can be transformed. All those things you'd like to ignore or sweep under the proverbial rug can actually add strength to your life if you allow the Light of the World access to them. You may have been taught to fear exposure, but there is complete freedom and great joy in surrendering to the Light. Just as the light of a brilliant sunrise sheds its vibrant glow on everything it touches, so too the loving rays of the Sun of Righteousness transform all who remain in him.

My sister and friend, it's tempting to keep hidden away those parts of ourselves that we'd rather not face, those areas in which we continue to fall, those corners of our minds that seem hopeless and helpless, but we *must not* move away from the Light!

Without fear, we can be completely exposed and completely loved by our God, who is Light and Life. Don't try to cover your sin with busyness, distractions (binge watching, eating, or shopping, anyone?), fantasies, hobbies, or even good causes and church service. Instead, open your eyes and heart to the Light who exposes darkness and then expels it.

Thankfully, neither physical light nor spiritual illumination depends on you. Light *will* illuminate; that's what it does in the world of vision, and—even more marvelously—that's what *he* does in your life of faith. Your diligence and your ability to examine and evaluate your own life is secondary (at best!). It is God who does the revealing, and it is his mercy and grace that superintends the process. Sad to say, if you and I tried to expose our own sin, we'd certainly deceive ourselves. In the light of love and liberty, even the smallest fault is visible, but this is no cause for fear. In the full exposure of God's light, you can be healed.

While I was suffering the ongoing effects of two severe postpartum depressions, my psychiatrist counseled me to spend an hour every day in the sun, preferably—he added—with as much skin exposed as possible. Weird advice? Actually, no. In order to heal, my body needed to absorb light, and the medicinal properties with which God imbued it. This idea may strike you as strange if you only associate the sun's rays with detrimental effects (aging, skin cancer, etc.), but light has traditionally been understood as a powerful healing force. That's why the people of Israel accepted Malachi's promise of a "sun of righteousness" who would "rise with healing in its wings" as a prophecy of their Deliverer, their one great Hope. His light would usher in perfect health, freedom, and joy (Mal. 4:2 NASB). Jesus fulfills this promise!

Light also provides heat and power in the physical world; likewise, the Light of the World provides the fuel and energy we need to live freely. It takes tremendous power and principle to enjoy freedom. Bondage is an easy path, but liberty comes at great cost. Just as people harness the power of the sun to equip their machines and meet their physical needs, we should look to the *far greater* power of the Light of the World to fuel our daily life.

Finally, light guides. If you've ever been camping, you know that light is necessary to make it through the night. Bright stars or moonlight are certainly helpful, but a fire and flashlight make things even easier. When darkness descends, you want to be near the light; it's for your own good, your protection and provision. You're not *required* to remain near the light or follow the course it illuminates, but you certainly fare better if you do so.

Jesus is a light that should be followed. Reading about his power to overcome darkness or knowing about the freedom from sin he offers is, quite simply, not enough. You and I must choose to follow the Light who guides. Light will expel darkness in you, but only to the degree that you receive it. In order to better open our hearts to the Light of the World, let's look now at some of the ways darkness clings to our minds and hearts.

Know Your Enemy

Jesus is the Light of the World, but an enemy who seeks your destruction opposes God's power on every side, prowling around "like a roaring lion looking for someone to devour" (1 Pet. 5:8). This enemy is known by many names, including the Prince of Darkness and the Father of Lies. It's so important that you and I know the enemy's tactics, the ways he seeks to undermine light and life in us. If we don't, we allow darkness to slip into our lives uncontested.

Your enemy will use several *D*s to keep you from the life Christ died to give you: delusion, deceit, doubt, deformed desire, division, and distraction.

One of the primary ways the enemy attacks "good Christian girls" is getting them to believe that their sin isn't *that* bad. "I mean," his lie goes, "it's not like you're doing _____ (insert whatever you consider a 'big sin' here). Sure, you're human and mess up like everyone else, but it's not *that* big of a deal . . ."

This may sound harsh, but such prideful delusion is the pathway to destruction. I know because I've been down this road. I've convinced myself that my battles with control and vanity weren't that big of a deal, and I ended up with an eating disorder; I've felt confident that I could handle reading those romance novels or watching those rom-com flicks and found myself fantasizing about fictional characters; I've justified being careful with my money to the exclusion of generosity and sacrifice; I've rationalized speaking directly to (aka yelling at) my kids because "they need to know that this bad behavior won't be tolerated." I have been deluded more often than I care to admit and certainly more frequently than I can outline here. My sin is prideful and ugly and *dark*.

You and I may be unconsciously tolerating a certain degree of darkness in our lives simply because we've been played. We've been hoodwinked into believing that the little things in our lives are just that—little things. God's Word blows the lid off this thinking: "Catch for us the foxes," it commands, "the little foxes that ruin the vineyards, our vineyards that are in bloom" (Song 2:15). Sometimes it's tiny things that infect us with darkness.

François Fénelon's eighteenth-century words pierce my twenty-first-century pride and delusion:

> We are more easily deceived about small matters if we imagine them to be innocent and think that we are indifferent to them. . . . "It is a small matter," they say. That is true, but it is of amazing consequence to you. It is something you love enough to refuse to give it up to God. It is something you sneer at in words, so that you may have an excuse to keep it: a small matter—but one that you withhold from your Maker, which can prove your ruin. . . . The greatest danger of all is this: by neglecting small matters, our soul becomes accustomed to unfaithfulness.[2]

I don't know about you, but I do not want my soul to become accustomed to unfaithfulness. I don't want to sneer at "small things" that I actually love so much I refuse to give them up to God. *That* is a perfect recipe for walking in darkness, if you ask me. If we are to live in light, we must reject the fallacy of small things.

Another method of deception the enemy uses involves lies about how and why we sin. The Prince of Darkness wants you to believe that sin is about *behavior* and that if you only found the right technique or tried harder, you could overcome it. This perilous deceit has mired many women in the deep darknesses of behavior modification, perfectionism, and denial.

The Bible teaches that sin is—first and foremost—a condition of the heart. If you believe sin is about behavior and behavior alone, you will work hard to clean up your actions and present a "put-together" picture for others (maybe even for God). My friend, this is doomed to failure. Jesus tells us that we *always* live—we act and speak and make decisions—out of the heart (see Matt. 5–7 and Luke 6:43–45). Sin infects more than just what you do; darkness casts its shadow over your thoughts, desires, and motives. As one pastor puts it: "Your body goes physically where your heart has already gone. This is precisely why we need rescuing Grace. We can run from a certain situation, location, or relationship, but we have no ability whatsoever to escape our hearts."[3] For that, we need the Light of the World. We need his gracious power to expel darkness from the corners of our minds, from the foundations of our motives, from the depths of our desires.

Sin is never simply the result of being in the wrong place at the wrong time with the wrong people. Sin is connected to the darkness inside you. Because sin inside of you acts like a hook that grabs hold of the darkness outside, you need rescuing from yourself. I do, too (more than you can possibly imagine!). We need light to guide us away from the lie that if we just got things together and did the right things, then we'd be "good little girls."

Another deception I've often faced is the idea that sin is about breaking rules. If this were true, there would be ways to "make up" (the biblical word is "atone") for my own mistakes. Sin is more than just the shattering of an abstract guideline. Every single sin breaks my relationship with God, not simply a rule. When you and I sin, we give something other than God power over our lives. It may be fear or anger, lust or greed. It may be love that's gotten confused or hope that's been too long deferred. Regardless of where it stems from, every sin injures my relationship with God because it's rebellion against his sovereignty, not just against his rules. Sin is *personal*. And that is why we need a *personal* relationship with God to overcome it. Don't be fooled! The darkness that threatens us is not an "issue"; it attacks the very core of our relationship with God.

Ephesians 4:22 commands, "Put off your old self, which is being corrupted by its deceitful desires." Delusions are all around us. False lights shine on every side. Learn to discern between the lies of the enemy and the true Light of the World. The enemy isn't omniscient, as God is. He can't read your mind or see the future; he has had, however, thousands of years to study human nature. He knows humanity well enough to predict with frequent accuracy when, where, and how you are vulnerable. Don't stay in the dark! If we surrender to them, the temptations of darkness at moments of particular weakness can have major consequences. Live in the light that God offers; his word is a lamp for your feet and a light for your path (Ps. 119:105).

It's often helpful for me to write down or say out loud the things swirling inside my head. Rapid-fire thoughts assault me and I need help sorting them out! God's light reveals lies like these in my mind:

- God doesn't understand.
- You don't *have* to . . .
- God's holding out on you.
- God doesn't care about what you want and he's never going to.

- You can't believe that promise; maybe that's for other people, but not you.
- If it's the right thing to do, it shouldn't be this hard.
- If God really loved you, he'd do _____ or wouldn't have done _____.

Through lies like these, the enemy attacks, attempting to infect us with the darkness of *doubt*. Getting you to question God's character—particularly his love, goodness, power, and provision for you—is one of the Prince of Darkness's favorite tactics. Be aware that he'll also try to convince you that you don't have what it takes to be a "good Christian" at the same time as he's persuading you to disbelieve God's character.

In the next section, we'll unpack specific ways to counterattack when doubts arise, but for now I want to encourage you with Romans 6:11: "You should consider yourselves dead to sin and able to live for the glory of God through Christ Jesus" (NLT 1996). Through him *you are able* to face doubts about who he is and who you are. You are not helpless or hopeless. Darkness has no power over you that you don't give it. Remember, when the Light of the World came on the scene of your life, he made darkness a choice. We'll look more closely at choosing to believe light and truth after we expose the final three strategies our enemy employs to keep darkness within us: deformed desire, division, and distraction.

For Christian women, the progression of sin is often one of deformed desire. We see this evidenced in the very first sin on earth. According to the biblical account, Eve "saw that the fruit of the tree was good for food and pleasing to the eye, and also desirable for gaining wisdom" (Gen. 3:6). In other words, she *wanted* it; she was *attracted* to it. Once the enemy had introduced the idea that the forbidden fruit was desirable, Eve began to think about it differently. The woman God created perfectly, the one who experienced life as God fully intended it to be, now felt that she lacked something essential; she longed for more. The idea that God had withheld something from her and would never give her what she really needed began to eclipse every other thought in Eve's mind.[4]

The pattern of sin is the same today as it always has been. Desire starts in the mind, and it may start innocently enough. The suggestion is made that you could—maybe even *must*—fulfill this desire for yourself. God certainly won't, the lie may go. He doesn't care about something like *that* or else he would have _____. You don't have to wait on him, the darkness may insinuate. The desire begins to grow and shove other thoughts from your mind. A kind of desperate urgency may press on you: you have to do something . . . *now* . . . it will suggest. Pressure will mount to address the ache of desire on your own rather than wait for or trust in God's provision.

My friend, desire deformed by darkness is *always* deadly. The enemy will twist your longings and loves—even for really good things—into something that controls and compels you. This is not the path of freedom. At the very moment that desire begins, humbly ask the Light to shine on it. Ask him to help you know whether this desire is pure or deformed.

Desire itself is not sin. That is essential to understand. It's desire that has been twisted by darkness that will prove your undoing. The book of James puts it starkly: "Each person is tempted when they are dragged away by their own evil desire and enticed. Then, after desire has conceived, it gives birth to sin; and sin, when it is full-grown, gives birth to death" (1:14–15). The original Greek word that the NIV renders here as "evil desire" refers to desire infected with darkness, desire turned inside out and upside down. Desires to be loved, accepted, comfortable, safe, and happy are not inherently wrong; they can, however, become deformed.

In a similar manner, the enemy will use distractions to spread darkness in you. He may manipulate circumstances to keep you busy or comfortable; he may twist trials that God intends to use to strengthen and sharpen you into sources of temptation to despair, fear, or anger. In other words, he will distract you in whatever way he can from leaning into the Light of Life. I find that distraction is one of the biggest stumbling blocks in my faith. I like pleasure and comfort and I really hate calamity and challenge. The more I give in to distraction—whether through excessive busyness or through physical pleasures (food, fitness, sex, entertainment, etc.), the more easily darkness of my own choosing obscures the way.

You and I must reject distraction if we're to enjoy the light of life and freedom from darkness. Your enemy will do everything in his power to distract you from prayer. He'll even use church service and "good Christian things" (Bible study groups? Faith-based homeschooling? Social justice?) to keep you from spending time one-on-one with Jesus. He'll make you think that your actions are more important than your own heart connection with Christ each and every day. The Prince of Darkness will prompt you to postpone or curtail your time with God; he'll introduce urgent needs or demands to keep your mind unfocused and cluttered. Don't be deluded! Your enemy wants to divide you from the light.

And thus we arrive at a final strategy of darkness, that of division. The enemy will certainly use whatever means he can to separate you from the Light of Life. He'll also try to divide you from fellowship with others. Bitterness, envy, resentment, anger, unmet expectations, fear, shame—really any strong emotion—can be utilized by the enemy to spread the darkness of division within you. When you feel distant from the light, when you feel alienated and isolated, allow God's light to shine on your relationships; you may find the enemy has been at work to divide you from fellowship with others.

Where Victory Is Found

Praise be to God, we need not despair when considering the weapons our enemy wields. God assures us of his ultimate victory! "The one who is in you is greater than the one who is in the world" (1 John 4:4). Greater is he who is in you . . . no qualifiers, no exceptions.

If you have chosen Jesus as the Light of your life, you are no longer under the curse of sin and brokenness: "He has rescued us from the dominion of darkness and brought us into the kingdom of the Son he loves" (Col. 1:13). What liberating truth! Others may stumble in darkness, "but you are not controlled by your sinful nature. You are controlled by the Spirit" (Rom. 8:9 NLT). Don't focus so much on the enemy's tactics that you forget to celebrate and rely on the greater power in you!

This power and provision comes not in the form of a tool you use or a weapon you wield. Instead, God gets *in* you with his light and life. Jesus transforms you from the inside out. The Holy Spirit is a warrior who works tirelessly to expel the shadows from your mind and heart. His redemptive zeal is unmatched and unstoppable. He will fight even when you don't care or don't recognize your need to.

In order to experience that transforming power, however, you and I must love light and hate darkness. Sad to say, many women have developed a taste for the dark. Whether through long exposure to questionable entertainment or swept-under-the-rug sin, some of us have accustomed our souls to the shadows.

Andrew Murray speaks wisely to this matter: "Nothing but the constant nearness and unceasing power of the living Christ can make it possible for you to understand what sin is and to detest it. Without this deeper understanding of sin, there will be no thought of appropriating the victory that is made possible for you in Christ Jesus and will be wrought in you by the Spirit."[5] Victory is found in nearness to the Light.

Darkness sometimes feels overwhelming, but that's a delusion of appearance. Obedience is the pathway to light, power, freedom, and *life*. The apostle Paul affirms, "The temptations in your life are no different from what others experience. And God is faithful. He will not allow the temptation to be more than you can stand.

When you are tempted, he will show you a way out so that you can endure" (1 Cor. 10:13 NLT). The trouble with this verse is that so often we don't want to take the way out he shows us. We want some other, perhaps easier or less painful way.

Half-hearted obedience doesn't unleash the power of light. Are you tempted to gravitate toward minimalism when God asks something of or from you? Do you wonder, "What's the least I'm required to do and the most I can get away with?"[6] If so, light doesn't yet have its proper place in your life. Jesus saves you, not by instantly removing every sinful impulse, but by empowering you progressively, teaching you to live in and love the light. Let's close this chapter with a practical look at saying yes to the light and no to the dark.

Practicing the Prayer of Confession and Repentance

Confession and repentance are two sides of the same, life-changing coin; confession pertains to our words and the state of our hearts, while repentance involves our actions. In learning to practice these, light gains victory over darkness inside us.

To begin, I encourage you to memorize and pray the words of Psalm 139:23–24: "Search me, God, and know my heart; test me and know my anxious thoughts. See if there is any offensive way in me, and lead me in the way everlasting."

These verses invite the Spirit of Light and Truth to convict you. As he reveals any darkness remaining in you, he also offers a choice. You can agree with God that what's within you is dark and acknowledge the wrong to him, or you can hide. Choosing the former, you can rejoice in this truth: "If we confess our sins to him, he is faithful and just to forgive us our sins and to cleanse us from all wickedness" (1 John 1:9 NLT).

True confession occurs when you align your thoughts with God's. To be perfectly honest, I cannot afford to think my own thoughts. I deceive myself so often. When I allow God's light to transform my mind, to shine on my motives, desires, and actions, he begins to purge the darkness from me. This invitation is extended to you as well.

When you are confronted once again with the darkness in you—when you see the ugliness and know full well that you can never overcome it—*right then* is the moment of most beautiful opportunity. When you scream at the kids, blow off your husband's sexual needs, feel the weight of not-good-enoughness, when it all comes crashing down again, you are invited to confess, *I need you, Lord. The darkness is too much for me.* Honesty is key here! "Healing comes only by walking with God through our brokenness, never by avoiding it and pretending it isn't there."[7] In a marvelous (albeit rather unnerving) way, redemption is found in exposure to the Light. Hiding is hopeless; sincere confession is the path of restoration.

Both confession and hiding are about alignment; you either confess your agreement with God's truth, or you line yourself up with something else. And make no mistake: *everything* apart from the Light of the World is darkness. You practice the prayer of confession by allowing your heart and soul to be exposed to light, agreeing with what God says about himself, about you, about what you've done or desire to do.

The next step, repentance, involves acting upon your confession, literally turning the opposite direction. In metaphorical terms, it's leaving the darkness and walking in light. After your heart has been cleansed through confession, you still have a choice to make: What will you *do* with the light within you? My encouragement to you is the same as given by the disciple Jesus loved: "Walk in the light, as he is in the light" (1 John 1:7). If you confess and repent, you will be cleansed from *all* darkness. Doesn't that sound good?

Questions for Personal Reflection or Group Discussion

1. Review the properties of light listed on page 100. Which is most meaningful to your relationship with Jesus?
2. Journal about or discuss the following: "By neglecting small matters, your soul becomes accustomed to unfaithfulness." What "small things" try to steal light from your life?
3. What is the difference between confession and repentance? Why are both essential to living in the light?

Recommended Reading

- Fénelon, François. *Talking with God*, trans. Hal M. Helms. Brewster, MA: Paraclete Press, 1997.
- Lewis, C. S. *The Great Divorce*. New York: HarperCollins, 2001.

{7}

The Unforced Rhythms of Grace

You would love my friend Michelle. She's the kind of woman you feel privileged to know: deep, thoughtful, passionate about life and love and the Lord, plus super fun to hike and bodyboard with.

Because she lives and ministers in Central Asia, Michelle and I don't get to see one another as often as I'd like. She comes home most summers and we squeeze in time when she's not visiting family or missions' supporters, but internet calling is often the best way for us to connect. Praise God for Skype!

During one extended catch-up, Michelle mentioned a book she'd been reading. It sounded interesting, but I wasn't necessarily going to order it the second we hung up. That all changed when she said, "Jerusha, I had the biggest 'aha' when I read this: 'Slaves don't rest. Slaves *can't* rest. Slaves, by definition, have no freedom to rest. Rest, it turns out, is a condition of liberty. God calls us to live in the freedom that he won for us.'[1] He calls us to rest, not to frantic busyness."

I felt all at once tremendously relieved and tremendously sad. Relieved because I'm not a slave—I've been set free by Jesus and don't have to work myself to the bone—but sad because I often live as if I'm only good if I'm productive, whether that's in my parenting or marriage, my work or ministry. In my often-broken thinking, rest has to be stolen or justified; if I've had a huge week, I may squeeze in a nap on Sunday, but even then I sometimes feel the need to rationalize it to myself and/or others: "I was just so exhausted I couldn't keep my eyes open . . ."

What would the world be like if we could just say to one another, "I take one day every week to do nothing productive; I rest and enjoy good food, good times with family and friends, and the goodness of God. I don't work; I don't even *think* about work. It's my day to remember that God can do more through me in six days than I can accomplish in 365 frenetically busy ones"?

What if we actually valued rest so much that we arranged life around it rather than trying to force it in the cracks of overbooked schedules? What if we lived as if Jesus's promise—"I have come that they may have life, and have it to the full" (John 10:10)—actually meant that we enjoyed the rich and satisfying experience he died to give us *here and now*, not waiting for eternity? Most of us tend to have harried and hurried days, not calm and content ones. God's prescription for this is to follow in the footsteps of his beloved Son. Jesus proclaimed,

> I am the good shepherd. The good shepherd lays down his life for the sheep. (John 10:11)

He laid down his life so you wouldn't have to run ragged. He died so that you could be free of endless pressures to perform. He gave up his freedom so that you could enjoy yours. He willingly surrendered his days so that yours could be full and rich and satisfying. Why would you live any other way?

The When, Where, and Why

As twenty-first-century believers, we usually take Jesus's statement: "I am the good shepherd" at face value and without much consideration. Most of us live in cities, far removed from grazing livestock and green pastures; we know little—if anything!—about sheep or shepherding. Even those of you who have worked with sheep haven't experienced shepherding in the same way ancient Palestinians did. That's why it's both essential and illuminating to understand the context in which Christ made these claims. When we know a bit more about what it means for Jesus to be our Good Shepherd and for us to be his sheep, we can better experience the abundant life he died to give us. If you want to know true rest and freedom, get in touch with your sheepish roots. (Hmm . . . maybe that's a stretch, but hopefully after reading this chapter you'll know what I mean!)

Let's start with a question: What does the word "sheep" bring to your mind?

I immediately think of fluffy white lambs, innocent and harmless, dotting rolling green hills in some storybook setting. I think of nursery rhymes and cuddly stuffed animals. Cuteoverload.com comes to mind.

What I do *not* typically think of: creatures so timid that a single jackrabbit hopping from the undergrowth can start a stampede, animals so easily beset by parasites that they've been known to bash their own skulls in as they attempt to rid their heads of nasal flies, or beasts so hardheaded that they will descend treacherous cliffs to graze on tiny patches of worthless weeds, even if acres of nourishing pasture are safely available to them on higher ground.

Dear friend, when God calls us the sheep of his pasture (Ps. 100:3) and Jesus refers to himself as the Good Shepherd (John 10), he's not dealing in strictly sweet symbols. As pastor Tim Keller brilliantly notes, "When the Bible calls him the Great Shepherd and us, sheep, it is a very important and very well meant spiritual insult."[2]

117

It's an insult, but one that's intended to spark in us humble gratitude for the guidance and guardianship, the provision and protection of our Good Shepherd. Jesus isn't being viciously sarcastic here. Instead, this insult is "well meant" because knowing how very much like sheep we are helps us come to terms with our desperate need for not only a shepherd but the *Good* Shepherd.

So what do you need to know about sheep? Sheep are—how do I put this?—pretty dumb and ugly. Former shepherd Philip Keller writes,

> The harsh, and unhappy truth is that sheep just aren't that beautiful—except at a distance and in . . . the viewer's imagination. Sheep are very, very stupid! They are incredibly stubborn! . . . They are prone to sickness, susceptible to innumerable parasites and diseases. Timid, helpless, fearful creatures, they move under blind compulsion of the mob instinct. . . . They are, when unattended, harsh and hardheaded with one another. They have a natural predilection to walk away, ending up in difficulties of a dozen kinds. They are easy prey for predators. They are a perpetual worry to their owners. No other class of livestock demands so much constant, meticulous care and attention. No, sheep are not naturally attractive animals; and neither are we![3]

Eek!

Sheep also cannot do anything for themselves. They are entirely dependent on the quality care of a good shepherd, and so are we! Sheep easily lose direction and cannot find their way home like dogs or cats. "Even when you find a lost sheep, the lost sheep rushes to and fro, and will not follow you home. So when you find it, you must seize it, throw it to the ground, tie its forelegs and hind legs together, put it over your shoulders and carry it home struggling. That's the only way to save lost sheep."[4]

Do you see why this whole sheep metaphor is a bit uncomfortable? We're like dumb, stubborn, helpless animals. Yuck! This flies in the face of my Western independence. I don't want to be compared to a witless beast with poor eyesight, prone to the infestation of parasites and easy pickings for predators. I don't want to think of myself as a creature that doesn't know what's good for her and has to be seized, tied up, and carried home struggling by someone who wants only what's best for me. Oh God, isn't there something else you could compare me to?

Apparently not. God really wanted to drive this metaphor home. Sheep are—biblically speaking—everywhere; the Word mentions them on over three hundred occasions.[5] At the same time, Jesus also emphasized how *good* he is at caring for and loving his sheep. This is essential, because under the eye of a diligent and attentive shepherd, sheep can flourish. They can be deeply loyal to a shepherd who tends to them well. Shepherded by a wise guide, they can restore ravaged lands. Sheep can be a source of great pride and joy to a shepherd who nourishes his flock, providing for and protecting them. All this—and more!—is precisely what Christ, our Good Shepherd, does.

Over the next few pages, we're going to look at some specific dynamics of our relationship to Jesus, the Good Shepherd. Guided by his words in John 10, we're going to see how spiritual warfare, busyness, and stubbornness keep us from enjoying the abundant life our Lord died to secure for us. Let's turn our attention first to the obstacle of hardheadedness.

What's Good for You?

Do you know what's good for you? If you do, how good are you at actually doing it? I know how important good nutrition and exercise are, but I'm not always the best at *implementing* that knowledge. Often, my stubborn adherence to ideas or routines keeps me from what I know is good for me. Other times, I just don't recognize what's truly best. I'm ignorant, like a sheep foraging among weeds rather than grazing in green pastures. Please tell me I'm not the only one who struggles with this!

I mentioned earlier that sheep often land themselves in the most preposterous and perilous dilemmas—on the precipices of cliffs, for instance. It's unfathomable how these little guys can get into such quandaries, let alone how they might escape. It is, quite literally, impossible for stranded sheep to save themselves.

Sheep also stubbornly graze particular sections of pasture past the point of nourishment. In fact, they sometimes eat straight dirt without realizing that the grass is gone. Younger lambs, especially, are known to mouth rocks, twigs, wire, mud, gravel, etc., none of which are healthy or helpful.

Here's the spiritual parallel: Whether you are young in faith or simply in a rut, it's tempting to stubbornly "overgraze." We need to eat from the whole of God's Word, not simply focus on the same passages or receive instruction from the same teachers over and over again. If we hardheadedly cling to routines of reading his Word or praying only in certain ways, we may miss green pastures in an area Jesus is trying to lead us to. I don't want to eat dirt when Jesus wants me to "come in and go out, and find pasture" (John 10:9).

How many are the pitfalls of stubborn sheep! Shepherds often found "sheep stuck fast in labyrinths of wild roses or brambles where they had pushed in to find a few stray mouthfuls of green grass. Soon the thorns were so hooked in their wool they could not possibly pull free, tug as they might. Only the use of a staff could free them from their entanglement. Likewise with us. Many of our jams and impasses are of our own making. . . . We keep pushing into a situation where we cannot extricate ourselves."[6]

It's horribly true: many of my problems are of my own making. Stubborn and self-willed, I push into things that I should steer clear of. Most likely, you can think of a time when self-assertion led you to distress and heartache rather than triumphant victory. I can too.

I know so many women who feel worn out and beaten down by life. They're tired and troubled and don't know exactly why. I have *so* been there! I've also discovered that I often end up in those thorny situations because I tried to push my agenda rather than waiting for Jesus to guide and direct me.

Like sheep, we often don't realize when the way we're taking is treacherous (over a proverbial cliff) or full of brambles. Our Good Shepherd *does* know, however. In John 10, Jesus tells us, "I know my sheep and my sheep know me" (v. 14). Could there be anything more comforting? He knows us and is known by us, even when we don't know ourselves. He offers us *abundant life.*

If we want to experience this life, however, we must decide how to direct our energies. Will we continue to push forward with what we want, when we want it, and how we see fit, or will we surrender to the will of one who knows us and knows *everything else* too? The former is the path of stubborn independence that leads to destruction and discouragement. The latter is the path of real life.

The only way for a sheep to surrender is to trust the shepherd. To trust the shepherd, the sheep must know his voice. Similarly, we grow in faith and confidence as we know Christ more intimately. When he calls you, can you recognize his voice? If so, follow it! If not, choose today to start listening more attentively. You learn his voice as you read his Word, pray (hearing directly from him and holding what you hear up to the light of Scripture), and fellowship with others (God's voice often comes to me through the people I love who also love him).

Jesus affirmed that the sheep who know him "will never follow a stranger; in fact, they will run away from him because they do not recognize a stranger's voice" (John 10:5). Are you spending more time listening to voices other than God's? Television, films, social media sites, books, blogs—even things like news and education—can introduce "other shepherds" into our lives. We must not obstinately assume that the voices of our culture don't influence us. Instead, we are called to vigilantly guard against and *run away from* any voice that doesn't line up with our Good Shepherd's.

Thankfully, there is a wonderful flip side to our sheepish stubbornness. It's called tenacity. With all my heart, I encourage you to cultivate tenacious love for Jesus. Invest all the energy that could be stubbornly misdirected into the positive channels of knowing Christ's voice and following it more each day. Instead of being hardheaded, choose to be resolute and relentless in listening to the Good Shepherd's voice. Being strong-willed isn't automatically negative. If you're a determined person, concentrate that power in Christ's hands. Instead of eating dirt and getting stuck on the cliffs or in the thorns of life, choose today to follow your Good Shepherd.

Easy Prey

Sheep have many natural enemies. Depending on location, wild dogs, coyotes, hyenas, or ferocious felines may prey on sheep. Thieves and bandits also lie in wait for an opportune moment. Because predators usually pounce on an unsuspecting flock in the dead of night, only the most careful and diligent shepherds protect their sheep from human and animal foes.

As the sheep of God's pasture, we too are stalked by a fierce and determined enemy. John 10 reveals, "The thief comes *only* to steal and kill and destroy" (v. 10, emphasis added). Destruction and devastation are his sole purpose. Your enemy and mine, the Father of Lies and the accuser of your heart, plays for keeps. He relentlessly seeks your annihilation.

Unfortunately, many women ignore or discount the enemy's desire to kill, steal, and destroy. We cannot remain passive as he seeks to systematically obliterate us! To be sure, we don't want to excuse willful sin or identify every difficulty as spiritual warfare. The trouble is, we rarely recognize how widespread the battle for our spirits really is. Every movement toward God's grace and goodness will be opposed by his enemy because the Evil One's *only* purpose is devastation.

According to shepherds, there is one sure place of safety for a flock: as close to the shepherd as possible. It's the roamers and wanderers who are picked off by predators. Separated from their shepherd, sheep under attack are often struck dumb with fear; these poor beasts don't even utter a plaintive bleat before their demise. The spiritual parallel is sad, yet true: many of us foolishly stray from the Good Shepherd and find ourselves under assault; we may become so paralyzed with fear and confusion that we don't even cry out for help; we simply crumple as the adversary pounces.[7]

To guard ourselves against the enemy, we must remain close to the Good Shepherd, and you cannot do that without spending time with him. No one can genuinely respect, follow, and love someone they don't know. If you are living on secondhand knowledge of God's Word and zero communion with him in prayer, now is the time to act. Your enemy wants to keep you distant from the Good Shepherd. He wants you to believe that Jesus's purposes for you are too difficult and his expectations too high. Nothing could be further from the truth! Your Shepherd's sole purpose is *good*.

Many women I know argue that it's difficult for them to discern the enemy's tactics or the adversary's voice from their own broken thinking. While it's true that we might not immediately recognize the Evil One's strategies, there are some guidelines for identifying his attacks:

- *The enemy drives while the Good Shepherd draws.* A group of tourists in Israel once watched as a flock of sheep entered the city of Jerusalem, followed by a man pressing the sheep forward. One woman turned to her guide and remarked, "That's funny; I thought the shepherd went ahead of his sheep." The tour guide responded, "Madam, that is not the shepherd. That is the butcher."[8]

  Your enemy will drive you and pressure you. He will badger and condemn. The Good Shepherd, on the other hand, invites; he convicts to bring near. God's *kindness* leads you to repentance (Rom. 2:4). His mercy draws you to new life, to forgiveness, to recognition of your sin and a turning away from that which kills, steals, and destroys. The devil will bully and intimidate you, but Jesus wins your heart with patient love.

- *The enemy exalts self.* The enemy often seeks to turn your thoughts toward your perceived inadequacies, unmet needs, and disappointed desires. Anything that makes you—your problems, your longings, your fulfillment—bigger in your mind and God's purposes smaller is of the Evil One. The more you focus on self, the less time you have for God. This is especially true when you dwell on things God has expressly forbidden—affection or sex with someone who's not your husband, for instance, or financial gain through (even slightly!) unethical means. Fixing your attention on the Good Shepherd's truth is the best method to fight these attacks.

- *The enemy is crafty and cunning.* In the wild, predators want to catch sheep off guard, capturing them amid their confusion. Our adversary is the same. He slyly and subtly suggests thoughts or presents unexpected opportunities. His strategies are indirect and intelligent, so we must have our wits firmly about us. Don't be dulled by the voices of this world, which seek to lull you into spiritual sleep. Instead, "Put on the full armor of God, so that you can take your stand against the devil's schemes" (Eph. 6:11).

When I'm concerned about spiritual warfare, feeling ill-equipped and pretty darn puny in the face of the enemy's lies, I remember these precious words from Isaiah 41:10: "Don't be afraid, for I am with you. Don't be discouraged, for I am your God. I will strengthen you and help you. I will hold you up with my victorious right hand" (NLT). We need not cower in fear as the enemy prowls around, looking to devour us. Our God is victorious! He has promised to help us and strengthen us. Not only does God secure our victory, he allows us to rest right in the face of the enemy who would keep us on the deadly and destructive path of busyness (Ps. 23:5). Let's turn our attention to the Good Shepherd's invitation to ruthlessly eliminate busyness from our lives, not so that we can be more productive, but so that we might rest.

More Than Good Enough

Many years ago, I heard someone use an acronym for "busy" that I'd never come across before: Busy = Being Under Satan's Yoke.

Perhaps you've heard this one for ages, but it was entirely new to me back then. As a young mother, I was astonished to think that my packed schedule might be less about God's glory than I thought. I wasn't busy with country club meetings or tennis matches, after all; I was serving God alongside my pastor husband, taking care of my little ones, and doing all the things good Christian girls are supposed to do. Doesn't God want me to give "my utmost for his highest"?

The simple answer is *yes*, but the more complex answer is this: what I consider "my utmost" is not always what the Good Shepherd identifies as such. More than wanting us to live accomplished lives, God wants us to live *available* lives. Even doing what we think of as "good things" for God can distract us from availability for his purposes.

We pay a high price to maintain our frantic lives, often managing not only our own schedules but those of family members as well (I could literally spend half my life as Mommy Taxi!). I cannot tell you how many times I hear women at church lament or laugh about doing this or that "when things slow down." Trouble is, no one ever seems to slow down . . . *ever*. And living beyond our limits leads to exhaustion.

If our bodies had a "check engine" light, we'd probably bang our fists on the proverbial dashboard instead of attending to the distress signal. We sleep far less than is healthy for us, we say yes to many more things than we can manage, and we promise ourselves that things will settle down after _____. We feel this in our very bones, we acknowledge it to others, but most of us don't do anything about it.[9]

In Swahili, the word for a westerner is *mazungu*, which literally means "one who spins around." Apparently this is how others see us: whirling ourselves dizzy, a flurry of motion with no real direction, busy without bothering to really ask why. Is this ever true of you?

Someone asked pastor Mark Buchanan about the biggest regret of his life, and his answer startled me: *Being in a hurry*. Buchanan observed that "getting to the next thing without fully entering the thing in front of me" robbed him of joy. "I cannot think of a single advantage I've ever gained from being in a hurry. But a thousand broken and missed things, tens of thousands, lie in the wake of all that rushing. Through all that haste, I thought I was making up time. It turns out I was throwing it away."[10]

The standard response to, "How are you?" is no longer "Fine" for most women. It's "I'm so busy." Despite our good intentions and resolutions, our lives seem to pile one obligation on top of another to the point that our entire experience is one gigantic mess of "have tos," "shoulds," "need tos," and "oughts." No wonder so many people are depressed and anxious!

How grateful I am that the Good Shepherd's plan for me isn't one extended obligation. Instead, he calls me to set aside time for renewal and rest. In fact, he considers it so important that he included it among the prohibitions against idolatry, murder, stealing, and adultery. It's absolute insanity that we think we can obey nine out of the Ten Commandments, but completely disregard God's law: "Remember the Sabbath day by keeping it holy. Six days you shall labor and do all your work, but the seventh day is a sabbath to the LORD your God. On it you shall not do any work" (Exod. 20:8–10).

Many of us are terrified of resting because we believe that we'll miss out, that life will fall apart around us if we don't keep things spinning, or that we'll disappoint the people we love (family, friends) or labor for (employers or church leaders) by choosing to say no. We fear that we won't have *enough* if we don't keep going: our kids won't get a good enough place on that team or in that activity, our house won't be clean enough, our work won't get finished well enough, and so on, ad nauseum. For many women, the very first waking thought is "I didn't get enough sleep," and the second that quickly follows is "There's not enough time to do everything I need to do today."

Author Lynne Twist takes this idea further:

> Whether true or not, that thought of *not enough* occurs to us automatically before we even think to question or examine it. We spend most of the hours and the days of our lives hearing, explaining, complaining, or worrying about what we don't have enough of . . . before our feet touch the floor, we're already inadequate, already behind, already losing, already lacking something. And by the time we go to bed at night, our minds race with a litany of what we didn't get, or didn't get done, that day. We go to sleep burdened by those thoughts and wake up to the reverie of lack.[11]

The devastating truth is, the more we focus on "not enough," the less fulfilled we feel.

The Good Shepherd always provides *more* than enough. Many of us heard or memorized Psalm 23 at some point in our spiritual journey. Few people, however, actually live as if it's true: "The Lord is my shepherd, I lack nothing" (Ps. 23:1). I propose that we don't live out this belief because we're so busy trying to fill our hands with the good things around us that we miss the opportunity to be refreshed. We think it's a disaster when our plans are disrupted or sickness strikes, but sometimes that's the only way Jesus can get us to slow down. "He makes me lie down in green pastures, he leads me beside quiet waters," the psalmist asserts (23:2). I have discovered the hard way—through being *made* to lie down by devastating illness—that the Good Shepherd actually does what he promises to do: "He refreshes my soul. He guides me along the right paths for his name's sake. Even though I walk through the darkest valley, I will fear no evil, for you are with me. . . . You anoint my head with oil; my cup overflows" (Ps. 23:3–4, 5b). Why on earth don't we take him up on his offer for rest?

Here's Why . . .

According to former shepherd Philip Keller, it's almost impossible for sheep to rest unless (1) they are free from fear, (2) they are free from friction with other sheep, (3) they are free of parasites, and (4) they are free from hunger. Oh how sheep-like we truly are! Like the timid creatures Jesus compares us to, our fears keep us from rest, relationship tensions cause us distress, the disease of pests prevents us from finding restoration for our souls, and trying to nourish ourselves leaves us restless with hunger. Keller writes, "The unique aspect of the picture is that it is only the [shepherd] himself who can provide release from these anxieties. It all depends upon the diligence of the owner whether or not his flock is free of disturbing influences."[12]

We've already explored how Jesus satisfies our hunger, calms our fears, and sets us free from the need to be "in." Let's look now at how busyness becomes a parasite that sucks our energy from the inside out.

Sheep can become particularly troubled by pests like nasal flies. These insidious creatures buzz around the flock, depositing their eggs on a sheep's nose. When the slender, wormlike larvae hatch (gross, I know), they work their way into the sheep's nasal passages and burrow into the flesh (double yuck!). Intense irritation and inflammation are the inevitable result. In a desperate attempt to rid themselves of these annoying parasites, sheep may beat their heads against trees, rocks, or posts. Some severely infected sheep become blind and others rub, thrash, and bash themselves to the point of a frenzied death.

Yeah, that's pretty freaky. Even scarier is the truth that distractions and opportunities, achievements and possibilities can buzz around me like flies. The idea that I could do *more* or *better* burrows like a worm in my head, hatching its parasitic insinuation: I *can't* slow down! Whether it's a niggling distraction or an amazing opportunity that's creating busyness, life without rest can torment us to the point that we feel like bashing our brains in.

Jesus faced many demands while he lived here. I guess I assumed he was perpetually busy. I'd never stopped to consider what Oswald Chambers wrote, "Just think of how amazingly relaxed our Lord's life was! But we tend to keep God at a fever pitch in our lives. We have none of the serenity of the life which is hidden with Christ in God."[13] Chambers continues with another radical truth: "A sanctified saint is at leisure from himself and his own affairs, confident that God is bringing all things out well."[14] Are you ever "at leisure," confident enough in God's *enoughness*, his provision and protection for you, that you are content and relaxed? If not, doesn't it sound good to move toward that rather than continuing on the exhausting treadmill of busyness?

To prevent parasite infestation, oil (often mixed with sulphur and tar) must be applied on a sheep's nose directly and repeatedly. I absolutely love the spiritual parallel here. God tells us that he anoints our heads with oil (Ps. 23:5) and Scripture repeatedly connects oil to his Spirit's presence. We need to receive the Holy Spirit's truth and comfort as protection from the parasitic busyness that slowly destroys us.

Apart from nasal flies, flocks also find themselves vulnerable to scab, a disease passed between sheep who press their heads together. When we are frantically rushing about, we often come into contact with ideas and attitudes that create distance between the Good Shepherd and us. Cynicism, sarcasm, disrespect for others, hatred, and prejudice are just some of the "infectious" ideas that can be passed between sheep who put their heads together. Thankfully, the remedy for this, too, is the fresh application of an oil-based mixture, and the spiritual parallel follows suit: as we focus more energy and time with the Holy Spirit, his oil of gladness (Ps. 45:7 KJV) will protect us from being contaminated by thoughts that cause us to wander.

If busyness can be equated with being under Satan's yoke, Jesus's invitation in Matthew 11:28–30 becomes even more marvelous. I absolutely love the way Eugene Peterson renders this passage in *The Message*: "Are you tired? Worn out? . . . Come to me. Get away with me and you'll recover your life. I'll show you how to take a real rest. Walk with me and work with me—watch how I do it. Learn the unforced rhythms of grace. I won't lay anything heavy or ill-fitting on you. Keep company with me and you'll learn to live freely and lightly." Now *that* sounds like the kind of life I might slow down for!

Practicing Sabbath Rest

This year, I began intentionally setting aside Saturdays to practice Sabbath. Before I started, I thought it would be this amazing, easy experience of pure joy. Instead, it's been rough. I had *no idea* how restless I really was! I couldn't have imagined how hard it would be for me to trust that those emails stacking up would eventually get answered, that housework would get done, those issues I fretted about all week could be resolved by God and didn't require my immediate attention. It ultimately occurred to me that one reason it's been challenging to slow down is that I unwittingly operated under several myths about Sabbath rest.

For one, I believed that I had to be entirely still all day. That is *so* not me! I don't want to be a whirligig of motion with no direction, but I'm also a fundamentally active girl. One of the great joys of my Sabbath practice has been reconnecting with play. I am only now discovering again how to be active without being driven. For me, this may mean going to the beach and strolling rather than exercising while I walk down the shore, or simply floating in the waves rather than focusing my energies on catching the perfect curl. It may mean playing a game without striving to win, or dancing without having to "look good."

Another subconscious myth I believed about Sabbath can be summed up like this: there are certain "acceptable" things to do while resting. I thought of these as Bible reading, prayer, sleep, etc. Those things are important and can be wonderful parts of Sabbath, but that's not it. Anything that draws you closer to God—in short, anything that helps you embrace *abundant life*—brings joy to your Good Shepherd. Remember, his promise is more and better life than you could possibly imagine (John 10:10).

Because of this, I made a list of things that have no specified purpose (things that weren't "have tos" or "shoulds"); I simply identified things that give me life. They included watching nature documentaries (especially about sea life . . . I love God's creativity on display in the ocean deep!), preparing leisurely meals (when else do I take the time to try an intricate new recipe or make a time-consuming favorite one?), and coloring. I absolutely love trying color combinations and seeing a picture come to life. Since I cannot draw (I'm not being modest here; stick figures are a challenge for me!), coloring someone else's beautiful creation brings me great joy. None of these activities will get me ahead in life; none are necessary. They just nurture gratitude and joy in me, and that is quite enough to be getting on with.

I used to think of rest as an escape from the tyranny of the urgent, but I've learned that true rest is about engagement, not detachment.[15] *God's rest is about moving toward life, not trying to escape it.* That's why we don't usually feel better rested or more excited when we've spent the whole weekend seeking entertainment that simply "takes us away" from the pressure of our daily grind. True rest involves pressing into and through feelings of restlessness so we can be healed.

That is slowly happening to me. I now look forward to stretching on the floor of my bedroom without making it about gaining flexibility; it just feels good. I love savoring *really good* coffee and take great delight in thanking God for it. I love not looking at my phone; the calls, texts, and emails can wait.

I can't convince you of this, my friend; I can only invite you to try it. Push through the discomfort that you may initially encounter. Do it because God *commands* you to rest. I am so grateful he set the example. Like a wise daddy who knows that a restless toddler will fall asleep if he lays down next to her, our Father in heaven entered rest to show us the way: "For in six days the Lord made the heavens and the earth, the sea, and all that is in them, but he rested on the seventh day. Therefore the Lord blessed the Sabbath day and made it holy" (Exod. 20:11). If God can literally create the *entire world* in six days, don't you think he can manage your stuff in six days?

Deuteronomy 5:12–15 repeats the command to rest laid out in Exodus 20 almost verbatim. The striking difference is the addition of a reminder: "Remember that you were once slaves in Egypt, but the Lord your God brought you out with his strong hand and powerful arm. That is why the LORD your God has commanded you to rest on the Sabbath day" (v. 15 NLT). You are free, my friend, free to rest. You can lie down in the Good Shepherd's presence, free from hunger and fear, protected from the adversary and from the parasitic pressure of busyness. Decide today to start practicing Sabbath; it's your right as a woman set free by God.

~~~~~

Questions for Personal Reflection or Group Discussion

1. Which aspect of sheep explored in this chapter intrigues (or frustrates) you most? How does it apply to your spiritual journey?

2. Journal about or discuss the difference between being *driven* and being *drawn*. How does each take shape in your life?

3. What most often keeps you from rest? How do the suggestions for practicing Sabbath strike you?

Recommended Reading

- Buchanan, Mark. *The Rest of God: Restoring Your Soul by Restoring Sabbath*. Nashville: Thomas Nelson, 2006.
- Goggin, Jamin, and Kyle Strobel. *Beloved Dust: Drawing Close to God by Discovering the Truth About Yourself*. Nashville: Thomas Nelson, 2014.

Selah

Introducing the Way, the Truth, and the Life

If you knew the precise time, location, and manner of your death, how would you spend your final moments? Would you request a particular "last meal"? To whom would you most want to say good-bye? What would you say to them?

The fact is, *very few* people know when, where, or how they will die. Those who do tend to make the most of their closing moments here on earth: their last meal, their final farewells, their parting words; each holds special significance.

Jesus's experience was no exception. His final moments were full of import and influence. Indeed, almost half of John's Gospel details Christ's last two days on earth. His last meal is described in vivid detail; his good-byes to family and friends are drawn with heartrending intimacy. And John chapters 14–16 outline the final words Jesus spoke to his disciples before his death. These are Christ's "famous last words," or—as theologians put it—his "Farewell Discourse."

Jesus knows that his execution will be both gruesome and divisive. He knows that struggle and grief will follow in its wake. He knows the disciples will be scattered. In full recognition of all this, Jesus chooses his last words carefully.

Imagine being surrounded hours before your death by people you know will betray and deny you. You might be tempted to scold them or "fix" the errors in their understanding. Christ is in precisely this position, yet the tenderness and compassion with which he addresses the disciples—the very men who will desert him in his hour of greatest trouble—is unmatched. He speaks comfort and courage to his followers, both the disciples who dined with him in that first-century upper room, and those of us who worship him twenty centuries later. In these moments, Jesus proclaims precious truths such as, "In this world you will have trouble. But take heart! I have overcome the world" (John 16:33) and "Peace I leave with you; my peace I give you. I do not give to you as the world gives. Do not let your hearts be troubled and do not be afraid" (John 14:27).

Jesus wants his disciples—and he wants us—to face the troubles of this world with peace and confidence. This settled assurance comes not from "within" as the world presumes ("Look inside; you already have everything you need"), but *entirely* from God. Only the victorious Son of God who overcomes death itself can give the human heart authentic peace.

Jesus has already identified himself as the Bread of Life, the Light of the World, the Door, and the Good Shepherd. He has shown himself to be the Resurrection and the Life. Now, as he speaks these "famous last words" to his disciples, everything comes to fruition. He declares,

> "My Father's house has many rooms; if that were not so, would I have told you that I am going there to prepare a place for you? And if I go and prepare a place for you, I will come back and take you to be with me that you also may be where I am. You know the way to the place where I am going."

Thomas said to him, "Lord, we don't know where you are going, so how can we know the way?"

Jesus answered, "I am the way and the truth and the life. No one comes to the Father except through me." (John 14:2–6)

In this, the culmination of his "I am" statements, Jesus speaks of eternal rest, security, and joy in his presence. He gives the disciples (and us!) a vision of heaven. And he also promises guidance, truth, and genuine *life* for the remainder of our days on earth.

The apostle John repeats the words "way," "truth," and "life" throughout his Gospel. Indeed, chapter 1 records John the Baptist's proclamation, "Make straight the *way* for the Lord" (1:23, emphasis added). We're also told that grace and *truth* would mark God's chosen one and that in him was *life*, and his *life* was the light of men (John 1:14 and 4).

The whole purpose of John's Gospel is to demonstrate that Jesus is the way to God. He testifies to the truth of Jesus as that way, and identifies the life every human desires is only and ever found through trusting Jesus as the way to God. I love how Jeanne Guyon describes this in *Experiencing the Depths of Jesus Christ*: "If you follow Him as the Way, you will hear Him as the Truth, and He will bring life to you as the Life."[1]

Before sin entered the world, God created man and woman to know perfect communion with him. They were close to him in every particular and knew no distance from his goodness, faithfulness, and wholeness. Disobedience and selfishness infected humanity with separation from God, an inability to perceive Truth (it was a *deceiver* and his *lie* that tempted Eve), and the inevitability of death.

In God's perfect plan for redeeming the world, Jesus comes to meet our desperate need for reconciliation, illumination, and regeneration. Jesus perfectly fits a threefold provision to our triple need. He doesn't merely show us the way; he becomes the Way for us. He incarnates truth so that he can indwell us and transform us from the inside out. He offers life to all who say yes to him and gives each of his adopted children the chance to spread life and love to others.

The Greek language maintains a marvelous tension in the construction of Jesus's statement, "I am the way, the truth, and the life." In English we read it as a series, usually separated by commas, and often perceived as three separate entities that Christ imparts to believers. The original text makes clear, however, that these dynamics of Jesus's personhood are inseparable; they build one upon another in power and potency. John uses a cyclical form of expression, a grammatical structure that emphasizes Jesus is the Way to the Father *because* he is the irrefutable Truth and the inextinguishable Life.

Jesus is the Way back into the presence of the Father from whom sin separated us. Jesus is the Truth that allows us to know the Father's heart. And Jesus is the Life who restores to our days here on earth and our eternity with him in heaven the experience of our Father's goodness. The three are inextricable. You cannot, for instance, believe in the Truth without walking in the Way; that leads not to life, but to inauthenticity.

Because of the richness of Jesus's declaration—I am the Way, the Truth, and the Life—we'll spend the next three chapters looking at different applications of what Christ reveals in this "I am" statement. This will necessitate somewhat of a departure from the structure of our journey thus far. For instance, this brief interlude will serve as the "When, Where, and Why" section (as used in previous chapters to set the context for Jesus's statements).

Since we won't retread this ground in each of the following three chapters, keep in mind that Jesus spoke this "I am" as part of his final words to friends he deeply loved, co-workers with whom he entrusted his mission, and adopted heirs with whom he looked forward to sharing eternity. It's pretty stunning when you consider it.

Because the path of this world is littered with many "ways," we'll spend the next chapter looking at how to make wise decisions—Christlike choices—in an options-crazy world. We'll discover how discernment and abundant life fit together on the way.

In chapter 9, we'll spend time looking at how truth impacts a woman's daily life. It's a particularly important topic for twenty-first-century women, for whom social networking and frenetic schedules often lead to inauthenticity and isolation. Learning to love the *real you* and to *be* the real you is more than a hashtag project.

Finally, in chapter 10, we'll look at the unique ways Christ created women to share life with others. Talking about sexuality in this context promises to be a wild ride, so hang on to your hats and glasses!

My dear friend, sin causes us to hide our true selves, but Jesus is our way of return; sin makes us ignorant, but Jesus illuminates truth. Sin leads to the death of everything we hold dear, but life restores. We need Jesus now. We need him *always*. In the masterful words of Thomas à Kempis: "Without the way there is no going; without the truth there is no knowing; without the life there is no living."[2]

Let's walk forward on the way, trusting in the truth, savoring life now and forevermore!

{8}

Making Good Decisions in a Choice-Crazy World

Have you ever been lost? Not, "I'm frustrated because someone I'm with won't ask for directions" lost, not "I botched a turn back there" lost, but "can't think straight, sour stomach, feeling desperate" *lost*?

Many years ago, our family traveled to Pennsylvania to visit my brother in his new home outside Philadelphia. Our Southern California girls experienced their first white Christmas, complete with sledding on Uncle Jonathan's very own hill. It was all rather magical.

And then there was the time I tried to find a famous cheesesteak shop after dropping Jeramy off at the Philadelphia airport. Not so magical.

Needing to get back to work, Jeramy left Philadelphia before us. Jonathan loaned me his nice, GPS-equipped SUV so I could see my sweetheart off. That I did, and off we went; it should've been a piece of cake to get back. If only Philly cheesesteak hadn't been calling my name . . .

Two backstory things you should know about me: one, I passionately dislike driving. In those "Would you rather?" games, I always stunned friends by choosing a chauffeur over a maid or personal chef. Two, I am—how can I put this?—not the best driver in the world. I'm no speed demon or risk-taker; I'm just not very good at it. One might hope that twenty-five years of driving would rectify this; alas, I'm still doing things like rear-ending motorhomes and backing into UPS trucks. Yeah.

So, with these true confessions in mind, picture me driving around Old Philadelphia, a city whose streets were originally designed for horse and buggy travel. Tentative SUV drivers don't fare well on these one-way streets and turns that, if you ask me, are more like cruel imposters.

At first I had the run-of-the-mill reaction to my difficulties: getting hotheaded, blaming the GPS, wondering (accompanied by my signature deep sighs) why I hadn't brought the wireless headset for my, at that time, *not smart* cell phone, and trying to get the phrase "recalculating route" out of my mind.

While all this was happening, I ventured into some parts of the city that were, let's just say, less than savory. I grew up in the LA area, so I wasn't exactly afraid . . . at least at first. After missing more turns and winding farther into the labyrinthine inner city, that desperately lost feeling welled up inside me. Perhaps if I hadn't been so hungry I would've been less emotional. Maybe then my insides wouldn't have squirmed like so many fire-breathing dragons.

I had put all my trust in the GPS to get me where I needed to go; the trouble was, I needed to be able to follow the directions it gave, and I wasn't equipped to do that when the route didn't make sense and one mistake led to thirty others. I ended up at a grocery store, called my brother crying, and bought a subpar cheesesteak at the deli. Not the grand culinary adventure I imagined.

Apparently the restaurant name I had looked up before leaving the airport was a popular one with a plethora of knockoffs. Plus, there are a thousand little cheesesteak shacks—no exaggeration—in downtown Philly. Every time I made a wrong turn, the GPS recalculated, sometimes based on an entirely different destination. I wasn't heading toward a fixed point, but chasing an endless stream of possibilities (on a soft hoagie with grilled peppers and onions).

In this instance, operator error was certainly involved. Today's GPS systems are more precise and my phone is smarter than I am (this is, at least, what my teenage daughters believe), but getting lost in a sea of options is every bit as possible and perilous as it ever has been. In fact, our world is so choice-crazy, I think feeling lost is making a comeback.

I browse in the toothbrush aisle and see various shoppers stuck in a loop of indecision. This one advertises 360-degree cleaning action, but this one claims to reduce plaque and whiten at the same time. Oh, and here's this one. I'm not sure what it does, but it's more expensive. Does that mean it's better? Sometimes said mythical shopper is me, looking at deodorant (Do I actually need clinical strength?) or produce (Do these other people really know what they're doing when they're squeezing and smelling melons? I feel like such a poser pretending I know what I'm about!).

These are silly examples, I recognize. Life doesn't hinge on whether you get a tasty cantaloupe or pick the right toothbrush. If it's a bad one, you'll throw it out or eventually replace it; maybe next time you'll hit the dental jackpot. True, getting an effective deodorant affects more than me, so it's kind to spend some time making the world a better place on that front, but it's still not going to significantly alter my life if I smell less than fresh.

Some decisions just aren't that important, even if there are hundreds of options from which to choose. Other choices, however, *do* radically impact the direction and quality of our days on earth. It requires tremendous wisdom and the application of an über-biblical-sounding word, *discernment*, to navigate wisely in our choice-crazy world.

If people use the word "discernment" at all, most use it synonymously with "wisdom" and almost exclusively in prayer or church contexts. You might have heard someone pray for "wisdom and discernment" when a big decision loomed and clear direction was needed. You may have been the person praying!

It occurred to me about a decade ago that I had no idea what I was actually asking for when I prayed that God would give me discernment. This troubled me, so I spent a year researching decision making, how to listen for and follow God's direction.[1] In the process I began learning to discern and discovered that when Jesus described himself as "the Way," he gave us confidence in both our ultimate *destination*—the Father's house (see John 14:1–5)—and in the unfolding *process* (see John 14:6) of making decisions along our daily way.

Because of his great love and his commitment to finish the good work that he began in us (see Phil. 1:6), Jesus does not leave us to fumble along the way. Instead, he promises to guide us step-by-step, and unlike a GPS delivering computerized commands to a nervous driver around an inner city, Jesus doesn't give directions, then leave us to implement them on our own. He empowers us by his Holy Spirit to do what he's directed us to do and superintends all with generous grace.

Hundreds of years prior to Jesus's claim, "I am the Way," the prophet Isaiah promised God would provide a way for those he loves. He described the Father's plan to direct his people: "Whether you turn to the right or to the left, your ears will hear a voice behind you, saying, 'This is the way; walk in it'" (30:21). Isaiah also foretold a time when God's way would become a source of peace and provision for his chosen, set-apart people:

> A highway will be there;
>> it will be called the Way of Holiness;
>> it will be for those who walk on that Way.

The unclean will not journey on it;
    wicked fools will not go about on it.
No lion will be there,
    nor any ravenous beast;
    they will not be found there.
But only the redeemed will walk there,
    and those the Lord has rescued will return.
They will enter Zion with singing;
    everlasting joy will crown their heads.
Gladness and joy will overtake them,
    and sorrow and sighing will flee away. (Isa. 35:8–10)

What a great promise: if we walk on God's way, sorrow and sighing will not take us down! We will be led with joy and gladness. I don't know about you, but I could use more joy and less sorrow in my life! Walking with Jesus is the way to experience that.

It's not enough to merely believe in Jesus as the universal way, however. We must make him *our way*, living out that belief moment by moment, letting his truth define our decisions, allowing the power of his life to become our very own. Unlike choosing a toothbrush, these decisions impact the core of who we are; they shape our identity. Because of this, listening to and following Jesus's way, given through the Holy Spirit's counsel, is a primary means of experiencing abundant life. Let's look at how we walk in that now.

Right Where You Are

Have you ever used a GPS system that starts with the command, "Proceed to the route . . ."? That drives me flat-out crazy! Usually it happens when I'm in a parking lot or on an unplotted street. Sometimes I know where I'm starting from and have a general idea where I'm headed, so this instruction isn't quite so maddening. Other times, however, I haven't the foggiest idea how to get going, and it's infuriating to hear that if I could just figure out the first step, I'd be on my way.

I absolutely love that Jesus Christ is the Way that begins wherever you are. Right now—at whatever point of experience, no matter what stains or scars sin has marked you with—Jesus is the Way to your true home, to your Father's heart. Just as you are, at this very moment, the Way is open to you.

What incredibly good news: The Way has come to you, spanning the distance between a Holy God and the people (us!) who continually reject him. C. S. Lewis allegedly halted a debate about what sets Christianity apart from other religions with one phrase: *grace came down.* Jesus came down, to us and for us. God didn't erect a spiritual ladder for us to climb up; he became the living Way.

Without a deep conviction of this eternal hope, we cannot proceed along the route. If you don't truly believe that Jesus is the Way *for you, right now*, the path will remain open, but untrodden. You and I may attempt a variety of ways to please God, but neither of us will accept grace from—let alone follow—someone we don't trust. Jesus's declaration, "I am the Way," brings you and me to a point of decision: Do we trust him enough to follow?

How Personal Is Your Personal Relationship?

When you think about it, it's rather odd that a good number of people who claim to have a personal relationship with Jesus don't expect him to speak directly to them. Perhaps they believe that God talks with "superspiritual" people, but the Almighty One communicating with ordinary folks? Even if they wouldn't verbalize it, many think, *That's ridiculous!* How sad that the enemy has so distorted the truth!

Indeed, the reason we Christians claim that our relationship with Jesus Christ is "personal" is precisely because it's a person-to-person connection, and an intimate one at that! In Scripture, this relationship is likened to a loving—not a resigned and distant—marriage. You can check out Ephesians 5:22–33 for a great description of this.

Right now, take a moment and consider what you truly believe about your communication with God. Get beyond what you know cognitively or assent to theologically; instead, reflect on what your behavior and your rituals suggest you believe. Looking back over the course of my faith, it seems ironic that for so long I didn't associate *listening* with confident faith. Yet that is the very heart of a personal relationship! If you and I believe that God will (and *does*) speak with us, we will expectantly listen for his communication. Do you eagerly anticipate his words to you?

As I've grown and continue to mature in my relationship with Jesus, I've discovered greater joy in listening for his direct and personal words to me through Scripture, through my senses, and through prayer.

Reading the Bible is perhaps the form of listening that evangelical Christians know best (and feel safest talking about). God speaks powerfully through the words of his prophets, the stories of history, the psalms and proverbs, the eyewitness accounts of those who walked with Jesus here on earth, and the letters of his apostles.

Wow! When you write out the literary scope of the Bible like that, it's pretty remarkable. I love that God speaks to artistic temperaments through the poetry of his Word, to the philosophically minded through deep theological ponderings, to engineers and mathematicians through precise detailing, to the kid in each of us through captivating stories. Small children can hear God speak through the pages of Scripture and the most profound thinkers can never plumb the depths of his wisdom and understanding. It's utterly breathtaking!

The Bible makes clear that, within its pages, people can hear God speak. It also promises amazing blessings for those who listen.

Isaiah 55 proclaims, "Pay attention and come to me! Listen, so you can live!" (v. 3 NET). Life is found in his Word. Proverbs 2 reveals this:

> My child, if you receive my words,
> and store up my commands within you,
> by making your ear attentive to wisdom,
> and by turning your heart to understanding,
> indeed, if you call out for discernment—
> raise your voice for understanding—
> if you seek it like silver,
> and search for it like hidden treasure,
> then you will understand how to fear the LORD,
> and you will discover knowledge about God.
>
> (vv. 1–5 NET)

Did you catch the threefold exhortation here? When we read God's Word, we're to make our ears attentive, turn our hearts to understanding, and call out for discernment. If we do, we'll know and rightly revere our Lord.

Perhaps today is a good day to ask God to lead you along this way. Maybe this is an opportunity to approach the Bible in a different way, as more than an instruction manual penned thousands of years ago. God responds to those who ask! He will speak to you personally through the pages of Scripture. Will you trust him to do so?

Perhaps you have read (or even memorized) Hebrews 4:12 at some point in your faith journey: "The word of God is alive and active. Sharper than any double-edged sword, it penetrates even to dividing soul and spirit, joints and marrow; it judges the thoughts and attitudes of the heart." Do you experience this when you read Scripture? If not, what do you think about asking God to help you? Don't allow another day to slip by without listening for God through his Word. As the New Living Translation (1996) renders Isaiah 55:3, "Listen, for the life of your soul is at stake."

The Way of the Heart . . . and the Gut

For some choices, there are clear biblical parameters. While potentially uncomfortable, making a decision about whether to lie, cheat, or steal isn't ultimately difficult. Right and wrong can't be debated here. Other issues, however, aren't quite as cut-and-dry. How do you graciously navigate a relationship with a family member who chooses an alternative lifestyle, for instance? How much money should you spend on a family vacation versus social justice? Because our world overflows with options and we're required—every day—to make decision after decision, it's essential that we understand how to follow Christ when the way forward isn't specified by chapter and verse. How do we walk in *the way* when we don't have complete clarity?

Fortunately, biblical discernment helps us with issues like these, times when our way forward isn't expressly identified by God's written Word. Understanding the definition of discernment helps in this regard. For the one English word translated "discernment," the Bible actually uses eight distinct terms (five Hebrew and three Greek), so for practical application, it's essential to look at the various shapes discernment takes.

In some instances, discernment simply means, "to observe." It can also refer to understanding, wisdom, or common sense, to insight and awareness, to perception and the ability to distinguish, to taste (as in "a discerning palette"), to the act of judging, making distinctions, seeing clearly, showing prudence, paying close attention, or carefully, diligently, and intelligently considering. Yeah, it's kind of a big deal. To be honest, it can also seem a bit overwhelming.

There's a common theme that brings it all together, however: discernment always implies a kind of life, a Spirit-filled way of thinking and acting that forms the fabric of an individual's life. Discernment is not a theory or a method as much as it is God's way of life, a means of growing into the kind of people who habitually make good choices. Every biblical reference to discernment involves humans listening to God and using their minds, emotions, and/or senses to make wise decisions.

Many Christians readily agree with the "mind" portion of that statement, but feel somewhat uncomfortable with the idea that God might use the emotions and senses to guide and direct us. I've discovered tremendous blessing in the study of this very issue. Knowing that the Sovereign Creator designed our physical bodies to respond to his promptings has helped me on countless occasions.

You see, God's truth is written both into the core of the universe and upon the very cells of our bodies. Your brain's neural networks, your heart's biological structure, even your digestive system have been designed to help you glorify God in making wise decisions.

We've all experienced a strong "gut feeling," a sense that we should do or say something (or not do so!) at a particular moment. As a young Christian, I believed that I should ignore or discount such sensations; they're far too unreliable and *human*, my reasoning went. The truth, however, is more complex.

God designed your large and small intestines with an intricate network of neuropeptides and receptors. Your densely lined digestive track continuously exchanges information, responding to input from your thoughts, emotions, and will. This is why we experience "gut feelings." Since the Almighty Creator wired us this way, do you imagine he might want to use this marvelous design to help us honor him?

We don't always understand why we feel a certain way about things, why an internal "beeper" goes off when we're faced with a decision, but God often directs us to alter direction by giving us a physical sensation. Of course, we shouldn't rely *only* on these feelings. Because worry and fear can also give us powerful "gut reactions," we must always measure our senses against God's Word. As we learn to discern, however, God's design of our physical bodies helps us, particularly in moments when, considering time or other constraints, lengthy prayer and deliberation isn't possible.

Beyond your gut reactions, God has also wired your brain with an "automatic" response network. The small but mighty amygdala, the portion of your brain that acts somewhat like a library, cataloging and organizing past experiences and the emotions that accompany them, is a central part of the neural system God uses to guide us.

Because your brain's amygdala functions as an emotional "first responder" to thoughts and experiences, it compels action. If your neural library is filled with truth, you are equipped to respond to stimuli—both positive and stressful—with godly decision making. On the other hand, if the catalogue of "thought books" in your brain is loaded with statements such as "I can't do this," "I don't know what to do," or "This is too much for me," you will distrust your God-given ability to choose wisely. The neural wiring with which God designed us teaches us to respond to physiological cues with alertness and focus, filtering them through the heart. This is why it's so essential that I allow God to expel toxic thoughts from my mind and captivate it with his truth instead (see 2 Cor. 10:3–5). You can let him transform you into a new person by changing the way you think too! Just remember, our minds and hearts are only as strong as the truth we live out.

I've often heard preachers comment that the Bible doesn't discuss the heart in a physical sense, but strictly a metaphorical one. It's not the cardiac organ, some claim, but the seat of the will, emotions, and spirit to which the Bible refers. This is true in large part, but—once again—digging into biological science helps us understand and proclaim the complexity and glory of God's design.

Your heart is not merely a pump that circulates blood. Indeed, your heart is in constant communication with your entire body neurologically, biochemically, and biophysically. In these ways, the heart significantly influences the function of your brain—the formation of thoughts and the experience of emotions—as well as your other bodily systems, all of which operate together to compel your actions.

151

Dr. Caroline Leaf has studied the interaction of the spirit and body for over three decades. Her research and that of other medical professionals shows that "the heart's neurological sensitivity points to feedback loops between the brain and heart [that] check the accuracy and integrity of our thought life."[2] Amazingly, God designed your heart with its own independent nervous system, containing at least 40,000 neurons, as many as are found in some centers of the brain. The so-called "mini brain" of "the heart acts like a checking station or conscience for all the emotions generated by the flow of chemicals from thoughts."[3] How amazing to see that science is just now discovering that the heart truly is the wellspring of life, just as Proverbs 4:23 describes!

It's incredibly freeing to realize that God can use your intuition and sensory experiences for your good and his glory. We don't have to suppress or ignore what we feel; we can learn to incorporate it in godly ways. Because gut reactions and thoughtful hunches are part of how God may choose to direct you, carefully listening to our bodies is an indispensable skill to develop.

Women, as a whole, aren't particularly good at responding to what our senses tell us. We often don't rest when we need to, try to convince our bodies that they're not feeling what they're actually sensing (*You're not really sad; you're hungry*), and so on. Many of us don't even breathe enough! It was radical for me to recognize that I rarely took a deep breath. I was virtually panting for most of my life, bustling from this to that and back again.

Pause for a moment and inhale slowly, exhaling while counting to ten. One deep breath restores oxygen to brain cells, enabling you to think more clearly and act more deliberately. You can spare ten seconds to breathe deeply throughout your day. Taking a deep breath isn't simply good colloquial advice; science confirms its benefits!

God made me, and most women, sensitive to external stimuli. I have more visceral reactions to thoughts, emotions, and experiences than my husband, father, and male friends; the same may be true for you as well. Where I used to discount this and try to "rule over" it, I now incorporate the input of my gut and heart into my decision making. It's both freeing and empowering to do this to God's glory. With the psalmist, I pray, "Thank you for making me so wonderfully complex," Lord (139:14 NLT).

Practicing Discernment and Listening Prayer

Whether consciously or not, you and I constantly assign meaning to our experiences and emotions; we want to understand *why* and *how*. We are relentless interpreters. Our minds were designed to organize, categorize, and seek patterns. These human capacities bring tremendous glory to God when surrendered to him, and practicing listening prayer is a wonderful way to experience this.

God promises to speak to those who will listen. "Call to me and I will answer you and tell you great and unsearchable things you do not know," proclaims Jeremiah 33:3. Are you troubled or weary from the weight of trying to figure life out on your own? God promises to tell you things you don't know! He also assures us of his presence along the way. "Here I am!" Jesus declares. "I stand at the door and knock. If anyone hears my voice and opens the door, I will come in" (Rev. 3:20). We don't have to do this life on our own; he will come in if we listen and open the door!

The trouble is, many of us are far too noisy, busy, flustered, or confused to listen. When we initially try to slow down and practice silence, it's scary; our thoughts are all over the place and distraction paralyzes us. I recall taking a prayer walk around one of my favorite sacred spaces in California's Sequoia National Forest. I wanted to listen (or, perhaps more accurately, I wanted to hear God, and knew listening was necessary for that), but found myself divided by thoughts I'm chagrined to admit, let alone publish. I was agonized and frustrated. *Why is this so hard, Lord?* I lamented. His still small voice responded, "Because you are out of practice, Jerusha."

Make no mistake: listening is a learned art. We all know people who are excellent talkers and terrible listeners. More often than not, these aren't the folks we call in a crisis. When we need someone to understand, support, and help us, we turn to those who can listen well and respond thoughtfully. You also probably confide your hopes and plans to good listeners. Have you ever considered that God might want you to become this kind of person for him?

Psalm 25:14 affirms that he does! "The Lord confides in those who fear him; he makes his covenant known to them." God shares the way with those who are close to him, those who listen to him with attentive respect. According to Isaiah 30:18, he wants this kind of relationship with you. "The LORD longs to be gracious to you; therefore he will rise up to show you compassion. For the LORD is a God of justice. Blessed are all who wait for him!"

Listening prayer, sometimes known as waiting on God, trains you to hear his voice in the stillness. Just as Elijah knew God's way by attending to the still, small voice (1 Kings 19:12), we know the way through waiting on God in quiet, patient moments.

Here are some general guidelines to get you started:

- *Listen for questions.* Pastor Mark Buchanan identifies God's curiosity as his "most underexplored attribute." Buchanan describes the Lord as "downright inquisitive, brimful with questions."[4] We see the evidence of this from Genesis to Revelation, and never more starkly than in the Gospel accounts, where Jesus's frank queries stun and shock. This cannot be because our Lord is ignorant or forgetful; *I* ask questions for this reason—because I don't know or have misplaced something in my memory—but God does not forget (Heb. 6:10).

  Jesus doesn't ask in order to gain information, but rather to engage us. Questions pry open our hearts and invite response. This is our loving Father's purpose in asking: "You can talk all day at me, yet it obliges me nothing. I can listen or not, respond or not. But ask me one question, and I must answer or rupture our fellowship. God's inquisitiveness, his seeming curiosity, is a measure of his intimate nature. He desires relationship. He wants to talk *with* us, not just at us, or we at him."[5] This is why listening—and engaging God's questions—form such a key component of prayer. Keep a journal or notepad next to you when you pray and spend a few moments listening for any questions God might ask. Perhaps something like, "What are you afraid of?" or "Do you want to be well?" He may lead you with queries directly from a Scripture you've read that day. John's Gospel records Jesus's interaction with his first would-be disciples (1:35–39). He turns to these followers and asks—pretty bluntly—"What do you want?" (1:38). He wasn't requesting information from them; he wanted to lovingly show them the state of their own hearts, the desires motivating them. Perhaps Jesus is asking you today: "What do you want? What do you *really* and *truly* want?" Honest answers to questions like these become springboards for tremendous spiritual growth and deep intimacy with Jesus. Listen for them as you spend time with the Lord.

- *Listen for the "real thing."* It's generally true that the more you know his Word, the better you will hear his voice and walk in the way. An interesting parallel in the world of finance arises here. In the past, bank tellers were taught to recognize counterfeit bills in (what I found) a surprising way. Instead of studying the different kinds of deceptions they might encounter, employees handled authentic money over and over again. They were trained, by constant use and continual exposure, to recognize "the real thing." A similar thing happens to us as we spend more and deeper time in God's Word. We recognize his true voice rather than being distracted by the enemy's serpentine hisses. If you want to grow in your ability to make wise decisions, invest time in "the real thing." You'll find it's far more difficult for the enemy to mislead or misdirect you from the way when you're able to discern his counterfeit ploys.

- *Listen for insight.* God often illuminates the mind and helps us sort our problems when we listen quietly. His Word promises that if we call out for insight and cry aloud for understanding, if we look for it as for silver and search for it as for hidden treasure, then we *will* find the knowledge of God (see Prov. 2:3–6). Instead of simply begging God over and over again to "Give me wisdom" or "Help me decide," take some time to listen in silence. Write down what you hear and evaluate it against Scripture. If you feel confused by what you hear, talk it over with a trusted pastor, mentor, or godly friend. God often brings clarity as we process what we're hearing with others who know and love him.

- *Listen to consolation and desolation.* Ignatius of Loyola was one of the first spiritual teachers and writers to discuss the importance of tracking our sensory responses and emotions. I referred to the practice of examen earlier, and this form of prayer can be very helpful in times of decision making.

  In addition, I've found that using a method Loyola enumerated—writing my response to each side of a choice—to be tremendously beneficial as well. This goes beyond making a list of "pros" and "cons." In this form of listening, you engage both imagination and cognitive reasoning by envisioning yourself on the other side of a choice: How would you feel, what would you experience, how would your relationship with God and others look if you did "A"? What about "B"? Jot it down or, if you hate writing, speak it into a computerized dictation program. Evaluate what comes out. Your brain—and the heart with it—wants to make sense of things. Your mind is trying to form patterns and make interpretations.

You and I benefit from taking time and creating space for God to speak to us in this way. If you notice that you feel greater consolation (connectedness to God's plan and peace, even if a decision is difficult) on one side and desolation (a sense of spiritual conviction and distance from God) on the other, you can make a wiser decision. Be aware; this is *not* simply about "what you'd rather" or what would make you "happy" or more "comfortable." Thanks be to God, sometimes his will does lead to pleasure and peace. Other times, however, he walks with us through a valley of shadow in this sin-stained world. Either way, listening to consolation and desolation helps us connect more intimately with the God who vows to walk with us, to never leave nor forsake us (Deut. 31:6).

- *Listen for steps to obey.* A missionary to India for almost forty years, Mary Geegh, wrote a brief yet life-changing book titled *God Guides*. The simple premise of her writing: "When man listens, God speaks; when man obeys, God acts; when God acts, men change."[6] In other words, life change starts with listening.

  If you do what you hear, and trust Jesus to sort out your mistakes, you will find greater peace. If you are listening to God and he prompts you to call that friend you had an awkward encounter with last week, don't waste inordinate time questioning whether God really wants you to make that phone call. He will always lead you toward love, forgiveness, and redemption. If what you're considering will lead you or another person closer to God or along his way, don't ignore his leading!

- *Listen without discouragement.* During some seasons of our spiritual journey, we may feel that we're not growing "fast enough." If we've failed in a major way, we may feel that we're spiritually crippled, dragging along God's path rather than running the race set before us (Heb. 12:1). The words of church fathers Augustine and Thomas Aquinas are helpful here. Augustine wrote, "It is better to limp along on the way than to walk briskly off the way," and Aquinas continued, "For one who limps on the way, even though he makes just a little progress, is approaching his destination; but if one walks off the way, the faster he goes the further he gets from his destination."[7]

Praise be to God, in the Christian faith, it's okay to walk with a limp; in fact, sometimes wrestling with God leaves us limping long-term or with a thorn in our flesh (see Gen. 32:31 and 2 Cor. 12:7). Don't be discouraged if you're struggling along the way; God's power is perfected in your weakness. When you are weak, he is strong (see 2 Cor. 12:9–10).

Resist running to a book, a blog, or even a good friend first. When the way seems barred and you don't know how to move forward, *listen* first. God's way is not a dark and dreary one, but a living and loving way. His truth leads to life. The heartache in this world—the pain in your own life—is not the result of God failing to act or speak. On the contrary, most of the trouble in our world comes down to people insisting on their own way rather than following *the Way*.[8]

Because of this, here's the honest question I must ask as I listen and the query I encourage you to answer as well: Do I really *want* to walk on the way? Don't let your response be a pat Sunday school answer or a sentimental wish, a pleasant idea you indulge in when things are going well. Instead, dive in and discover whether you truly mean it. Do you *want* to do his will? Do you *want* to be led? Walking in your own way will not lead to truth and life. The human condition results in a wayward stumble, not a purposeful journey. Choose this day in which way you'll walk and listen. Jesus confides in those who attend to his still, small voice.

Questions for Personal Reflection or Group Discussion

1. Do you expect Jesus to communicate with you personally? If so, how? If not, why not?
2. According to God's design for our bodies, how can we use our senses to walk in his way?
3. Is it easy or difficult for you to be silent? What small step toward listening more are you willing to take along the way?

Recommended Reading

- Geegh, Mary. *God Guides*. Zeeland, MI: Mission Partners India, 1995.
- Willard, Dallas. *Hearing God: Developing a Conversational Relationship with God*. Downers Grove, IL: InterVarsity Press, 2012.

{9}

Discovering (and Loving!) The Real You

Nicole and Colby's wedding started in forty-five minutes. I was speeding down Highway 1 on my way to their swanky Malibu affair, pink sponge curlers bouncing in my hair (yes, some people still use these). It was ninety degrees this particular July afternoon, and I was sweating none so delicately. Inwardly grateful I had opted not to do my hair or put my dress on until I neared the final stretch of coastline before the Malibu cliffs ascended above the crashing Pacific, I scanned the road for a likely place to change (in other words, somewhere to commandeer a bathroom). A nice-ish Shell station on the right-hand side looked promising, so I pulled the green Honda Accord I'd borrowed from my parents into the parking lot. As I gathered my things and stuck my foot out the door, I realized with dismay that I had forgotten my shoes. I was wearing—go figure—the tackiest flip-flops I owned, the kind you sport around the house long after the flap peels away and the straps thin ominously.

Eek! There was no chance these were going to fly at a Malibu wedding. I hurriedly grabbed my cell phone and dialed my sister, who lived nearby in Santa Monica.

"Jess, is there a mall anywhere near . . .?" I described my location to her. She hopped on her computer and found a Payless shoe store not too far away. All right, it would have to do. Hopefully I could find some shoes that would look halfway decent. I ran into Shell's bathroom, yanked the curlers out, calmed the ringlets into a respectable wave and put on my dress.

Six miles out of my way, I located the shoe store and dashed inside. Fortunately, strappy white dress sandals were on sale and only half a size too small. I paid the twenty bucks somewhat grudgingly, but, on the whole, felt I had escaped unscathed.

The wedding was every bit as classy as I had imagined. More so, in fact. Still, no amount of swank could alter the temperature, and the eager July sun beat down on the glamorous and unglamorous alike. I sat, patiently awaiting the bridal march, well aware that I do not "glisten" or "perspire" like some females. I flat-out *sweat*. Really I should all-caps that. Armed with a cocktail napkin, I dabbed furiously at the beads forming on my brow and cheekbones. This went on for the entirety of the service, blessedly a short one.

After the vows and the kiss and the triumphant recessional, I chatted with some family members and friends of the couple. I didn't know many people, so I just tried to be generally friendly, talking to those standing around the hors d'oeuvre and beverage tables.

Before dinner began, I ducked into the ladies' room to wash my hands. When I looked into the mirror, however, I gasped with alarm. Perhaps you recall that I had been using a cocktail napkin to hold back the tide of my sweat. Well, said napkin was red. Said napkin was also strewn around my face in splotches of damp, ruddy cotton. Apparently no one I'd been conversing with felt they knew me well enough to tell me I had patches of red napkin stuck to my face. Seriously, people?!

The ordeal was embarrassing, but not tragic. I peeled the napkin off and decided laughing would be better than adding post-crying mascara stains to my humiliation. That said, I emerged from the bathroom determined to avoid anyone I had talked to previously.

Years later, as I was studying authenticity, I realized how often and how desperately I've tried to avoid napkin on my face. Not literally, of course, but in a metaphorical sense. I don't want people to see me sweat; I don't want to be exposed; I don't want to feel foolish or incompetent. I want to be the perfectly-put-together guest at the Malibu wedding, not the one in half-a-size-too-small Payless shoes with red napkin splotching her cheeks and forehead.

At some time and in some way or another, though, every woman has had napkin on her face. We try our best to hide what we see as our weaknesses or mistakes (my propensity to sweat, for instance), but covering up actually leaves us with figurative patches on our face and heart.

When Jesus proclaimed himself "the Way, the Truth, and the Life" (see John 14:6), he called us to mirror his character. If he is *the Truth*, we are to be truthful and live out truth as well. This involves risk and vulnerability (and sometimes allowing people to see us sweat). If we're to experience the abundant life Christ died to give us, we have to walk truthfully along the way, so if you're ready to ditch the red napkins in your life, the things you've tried using to cover up your weaknesses, join me in discovering and learning to love what's *real*, including the real you.

Finding Yourself (and Other Myths)

When I was in high school and college, people placed a good deal of emphasis on "finding yourself." I was encouraged, though I can't recall if this was tacitly or overtly, that finding myself was a primary aim. The message I took away from quasi-inspirational school assemblies was that, if I didn't find myself, I was doomed to suffer a life of unfulfilled work and relationships; I'd be destined simply to bide my time until a volcanic explosion midlife, during which I might have a second opportunity to discover my true self. Yikes!

The church I attended didn't exactly counter the "find yourself" rhetoric so prevalent in the wider cultural contexts in which I moved. In fact, some youth group talks used the same words, placing a spiritual spin on them and emphasizing that finding myself actually meant finding God. While there was some truth in this, I spent far too much time between ages fifteen and twenty-five looking at me and not nearly enough time looking at Jesus.

I can always trust C. S. Lewis to have something brilliant to say about virtually any subject, and the search for self and identity is no exception. In his master work, *Mere Christianity*, Lewis writes of the "new self" formed at conversion, the new self described in 2 Corinthians by Paul: "Anyone who belongs to Christ has become a new person. The old life is gone; a new life has begun!" (5:17 NLT). In conclusion to his brilliant apologetic for the Christian faith, Lewis articulates,

> Your real, new self . . . will not come as long as you are looking for it. It will come when you are looking for Him. Does that sound strange? The same principle holds, you know, for more everyday matters. Even in social life, you will never make a good impression on other people until you stop thinking about what sort of impression you are making. . . . Look for yourself and you will find in the long run only hatred, loneliness, despair, rage, ruin, and decay. But look for Christ and you will find Him, and with Him everything else thrown in.[1]

Look for yourself and find only loneliness, despair, and ruin? *Really?* Isn't that a bit extreme, I wondered?

Then I thought about the women I know who are most obsessed with themselves, with their accomplishments or parenting or even their spiritual status. Often, they're the very same women I'll later find out are desperately isolated and afraid, wasting away inside while frantically trying to prove themselves. In my experience, some of the loneliest women I know are the ones most often posting über-happy photos on social media sites. Strange how the search for yourself can lead to a constant need to be "liked" (or "favorited," or whatever is the latest method of digital validation).

I've never heard a sermon preached on it, but I believe Matthew 6:33, "Seek first his kingdom and his righteousness, and all these things will be given to you as well," applies every bit as much to our identities as it does to our physical needs. When we make the kingdom of God our primary concern, when we fix our eyes on him, the strength we need and the significance we seek are "given as well."

Your true self *is* worth discovering and loving, but you cannot find yourself apart from the Truth. Our great and glorious God promises, however, that when we discover and live in truth, we get to experience "immeasurably more than all we ask or imagine" (Eph. 3:20). The life I (carefully!) plan for myself too often ends in red napkin disaster. When I'm caught up in the greater good of God's will—his perfect and pleasing will, as Romans 12:2 affirms it to be—I "grasp how wide and long and high and deep is the love of Christ, and to know this love that surpasses knowledge—that [I] may be filled to the measure of all the fullness of God" (Eph. 3:18–19). Filled to the measure of fullness, with love that surpasses knowledge . . . now that's the *real me* I want to be.

"To Be Rather Than to Seem . . ."

So proclaims the state motto of North Carolina. It's a phrase taken from Cicero's "On Friendship," and the full sentence reads, *"Virtute enim ipsa non tam multi praediti esse quam videri volunt."* For those of us who missed Latin for, I don't know, our whole lives, here's a couple English renderings to chew on: "Not nearly so many people want actually to be possessed of virtue as want to appear to be possessed of it" or "Fewer possess virtue, than those who wish us to believe that they possess it."[2]

Seeming rather than being is, sadly, the focus of our day. We in the Western world have become extremely skilled at living behind a façade perpetuated by our digital profiles. We wear masks carefully constructed from posts, comments, pictures, thumbs-up (or thumbs-down), and emoticons. Some time ago, people started tagging photos as "no filter" or "the real me" because nearly everyone expected that things posted online had been neatly edited to fit the desired image of the poster. In a way, #nofilter was just another way of saying, *Look at me! I'm so authentic. Like me, please.*

Philip Keller writes,

> We try to present a brave front to the world, even though within we may be shattered, broken people. We proceed on the assumption that most people really don't know us and don't care. We often run a bluff on others, based on the premise that they will not or cannot be bothered to really find us out. The net result is that for many, life becomes a sham. It is almost playacting. It is played by people playing little games with each other. . . . It lacks depth, honesty, or sincerity.[3]

Our world has gone plastic, and so have many women's identities, molded to please everyone but lacking real truth and life. Our words, too, have become malleable, arranged in witty quips and 144-character sound bites. Such a world is particularly vulnerable to those who the apostle Peter claims "will bring the way of truth into disrepute" (2 Pet. 2:2). "Fabricated stories" will mislead people, Peter predicts, and God's very own will be "exploited" (see 2 Pet. 2:3). The Greek word translated as "fabricated" in this context is *plastos*, which is the root of our English word "plastic." A life that can be twisted and shaped into the appearance of something rather than the substance of it is dangerous and destructive.

It's dangerous because it keeps us from authentic communion with the Source of our hope and truth. It's destructive because always trying "to appear" or "to seem" is a terrible weight to bear. No matter how many mental lists we make of our successes and others' failures, none of us will ever be a perfect worker, friend, daughter, wife, or mother. Even if we do fairly well, most of us can't entirely quiet the voice of a conscience that sometimes screams, "You rotten hypocrite!" Women may respond to this by frantically trying harder; they may smear "concealer" on the uglier parts of life. Others simply give up. No matter what path we choose, self-condemnation leaves us frustrated with and alienated from ourselves, one another, and God.

Into our hiding and pretending, at the very depth of our confusion and bewilderment about being and seeming, God meets us with the good news: "I know you! I understand you! Before a word is on your tongue, I know it completely! I am before and behind you, and nothing is hidden from me!" (see Psalm 139 and Hebrews 4:13). Without apology, but with incredibly generous grace, the Lord exposes our pretenses. "Where can I go from your Spirit?" King David once asked. "Where can I flee from your presence? If I go up to the heavens, you are there; if I make my bed in the depths, you are there. If I rise on the wings of the dawn, if I settle on the far side of the sea, even there your hand will guide me, your right hand will hold me fast" (Ps. 139:7–10).

For some, knowing that God is intimately aware of the battle inside us between seeming and being feels nothing short of terrifying. But I have described it as good news because I know it to be so. I've been broken and exposed and have discovered that living in truth is better than I could ask for or imagine. *Being rather than seeming sets us free.* That he knows me so completely and loves me entirely (and at the same time!) comes as a great relief. If I don't have to perform for him, I don't have to perform for anyone. At last I can step out of the shadows of my own making and into the full splendor of his revealing love.

Come Out, Come Out, Wherever You Are . . .

For me, the process of being broken was neither pleasant nor planned. I wouldn't wish the course of my life on my worst enemy, but I do hope the ultimate outcome for every person I love. The result of brokenness in my life—the coming-to-grips with my own weakness rather than trying to escape it or turn it into something I can more readily accept—has been worth every moment of pain. Still, painful it has been.

I remember singing a popular worship song when I was in my late teens: "Brokenness, brokenness, is what I long for. Brokenness is what I need. Brokenness is what You want from me."[4] I had *no clue* that would involve years of struggle with mental health issues.

My battle with depression first became evident after I delivered our eldest daughter, though looking back across the course of my childhood and adolescence, I now see stirrings of the oncoming storm. At a time when I believed everything would be (or at least *should be*) happiest—after our healthy baby girl was born—I became virtually catatonic. I was beyond miserable; a shadow fell over my heart, numbing me deep inside. I remember hearing my husband, my friends, or my mom ask me questions or say reassuring things, but it all sounded distant and phony. The only thing that felt real were the hours I spent staring at the clock or ceiling while everyone—my gorgeous two-month-old included—slept peacefully. Raw emptiness haunted my daytime hours. It was the closest to hell I've ever been, and prayerfully ever will be, here on earth. I felt alienated from everyone and everything that once brought me joy. Hopelessness and helplessness so consumed me that doctors committed me to a mental hospital. Yeah. Bad day for a pastor's wife. Bad day for *anyone*.

I was actually one of the lucky ones, though. My postpartum depression responded rapidly to treatment, and within several weeks I felt closer to the Lord and more joyful than I had in my entire life. I gladly told people, "I wouldn't want to repeat what

I've gone through, but I also wouldn't want to trade the intimacy with Jesus I have now."

When I got pregnant four months later, I never imagined God would use postpartum depression to refine me again. Naïvely, I believed I had "learned my lesson" and would do everything "right" this time. I look back on that me and wish I could just hug her; I was doing the best I could, I suppose, but I was also woefully unprepared for the ongoing brokenness God allowed.

I delivered our second daughter with a shout of joy (literally) and experienced a couple months of ecstatic new mommyhood. *This* is what it's supposed to be like, I assumed. Then my milk dried up virtually overnight, and the huge hormonal shifts of plummeting neurochemicals left me mentally and physically adrift. It's a far longer story, and I've detailed it elsewhere,[5] so I'm going to skip ahead. I ended up in the psych ward *again*; I battled *again*; I sought medical help and counseling *again*, and God drew me up out of the pit *again* (see Psalm 40).

My story still hadn't reached its climax, however. Years later, while under treatment for severe daily headaches, my adrenal system began to shut down. Unbeknownst to me, I had been taking the crushed-up adrenal glands of cows. I had placed my trust entirely in the naturopathic doctor I was seeing and foolishly hadn't looked into the "prescriptions" he made, assuming "all natural" meant "100 percent safe." My body began to rely on this substitute hormone and my own adrenal glands went dormant. This was, needless to say, not a great situation for a person with tenuous mental health.

It was during this time, nearly ten years ago, that I was diagnosed with Bipolar II. Even typing that today brings up a number of disruptive emotions. There are so many ways in which I *do not* want this to be part of my story. Talk about red napkin disasters! A psychiatrist had told Jeramy and I during my first episode of postpartum depression that "you need to be aware that the severity of your condition means you could be at risk for mania and depression later in life," but I didn't actually believe I'd ever develop bipolar disorder. How could I? I was a *Christian*, for goodness' sake. Shouldn't my faith make suffering from manic depression an impossibility? Shouldn't growing spiritually make all this brokenness go away once and for all?

Turns out that brokenness, surrendering everything to God, cannot happen on my terms; it must occur on *his*. Furthermore, I cannot become whole again on my own terms. These too must be surrendered to him. A quote from Brennan Manning's book *Abba's Child* articulates this beautifully: "Wholeness is brokenness owned and thereby healed."[6] Wholeness is not, as I assumed, that moment when I "got over" all my issues and "dealt with" all my wounds; instead, it was the moment when I said an unqualified *yes* to God's fullness rather than my own competence.[7]

The myth of "arrival" is, tragically, still a powerful false narrative in Christian circles. It's hard for some people to hear me speak about my *ongoing* mental health issues; they would prefer things to be "solved" and assume that if I walked closely enough with Jesus, bipolar would be overcome by my relationship with him. None of us want battles with marital strife, financial difficulties, wayward kids, or past wounds hijacking our present lives to *continue*. We prefer focusing on the more-than-conquerors and victorious-over-all-things parts of the Bible. We want to *move on*; we want strength, not weakness—wholeness, not brokenness. These aren't bad or untrue hopes, but often they're based on assumptions grounded in human logic rather than divine grace.

Scottish pastor Andrew Murray's observations on this point have been both challenging and life-giving for me. He writes,

> The Christian often tries to forget his weakness; God wants us to remember it, to feel it deeply. The Christian wants to conquer his weakness and to be freed from it. . . . The Christian thinks his weakness is his greatest hindrance in the life and service of God; God tells us that it is the secret of strength and success. It is our

weakness, heartily accepted and continually realized, that gives us our claim and access to the strength of him who has said, "My strength is made perfect in weakness" (2 Cor. 12:9). . . .[Jesus] does not, as so many believers imagine, take the feeble life he finds in them and impart a little strength to aid them in their feeble efforts. . . . When he strengthens them, it is not by taking away the sense of feebleness, and giving in its place the feeling of strength. By no means. But in a very wonderful way *leaving and even increasing* the sense of utter impotence, he gives them along with it the consciousness of strength in him. . . . The feebleness and the strength are side-by-side; as the one grows, the other too, until they understand the saying, "When I am weak then am I strong." [8]

Of course I'd like to "get over" my weakness. I'd like to "be done with" my brokenness. And someday God may, indeed, entirely heal me from bipolar disorder. My sister and friend, in that very moment (which would be a glorious moment for me!), I will *still* be weak. It's an erroneous expectation to believe that we'll somehow graduate from our need for strengthening and transforming grace. Neither you nor I ever will. Instead, as we allow our feebleness to be caught up in his strength, we can proclaim, with the great cloud of witnesses who worship at God's throne, "When I am weak then I am strong" (2 Cor. 12:10).

Instead of simply seeking to "get through" your trials or "overcome" your weaknesses, instead of hiding your brokenness behind a digital front of filtered photos and plastic posts, come out. Come out, come out, wherever you are. I have lived for many years now with no skeletons in my closet, and I can tell you that it's absolutely the most freeing thing in the world to live fully exposed by God's grace and for his glory. I don't glamorize my weaknesses and I don't encourage you to do so either; that's one mistake well-intentioned Christians sometimes make when they're practicing authenticity. Being real doesn't mean that you share your deepest wounds and darkest sins with every passerby.

Instead, I'd like you to think of authenticity as integration, being the same exact person in every part of your life. Imagine this: the person you are at the mall is the same person you are at church is the same person you are when the traffic is so bad that the Bible's pronouncements on controlling your tongue are burning inside you.

Here's a visual that has helped me sort this out. It was first shown to me by Dr. Lisa Bode, an amazing counselor[9] who walked with me soon after my bipolar diagnosis and also four years later, when I had another breakdown. Dr. Bode introduced me to the graphic below, "The Johari Window." Those who first developed this conceptualization claimed that the human soul is comprised of four quadrants[10]:

Figure #1: The Johari Window

	Known to self	Not known to self
Known to others	Open	Blind Spots
Not known to others	Façade	Unknown

As you can see, the first quadrant is "open" and represents those areas of life that are known both to self and to others. These are the clearly visible parts of us, and usually things that we have come to accept about ourselves (even if some are less than desirable).

The second quadrant is labeled "blind spots" because these are the areas of our lives that others see but we do not. At some point, most of us experience a painful "aha," a moment when we realize that everyone else has been aware of something to which we were entirely blind. Not exactly a brilliant day when that happens.

Quadrant three is known to self, but not known to others. This is labeled "façade," for this is the area we hide. These are the parts of our heart that we try desperately to cover up, excuse, and deny. The façade keeps us playacting and posing. It's the false self we create to protect us from the pain of brokenness and vulnerability.

Traditionally, quadrant four has been deemed "unknown," and it corresponds to those aspects of self that are known neither to others nor to ourselves. For believers, I believe this quadrant should be renamed, "known by the Holy Spirit," for God promises that he understands and responds to even our indecipherable groans. (See Romans 8:26, one of my favorite biblical promises and, incidentally, one of the verses a charge nurse printed out for me when I lay immobilized in the psych ward; his name was Thor. Not a joke, though I gotta give props to God and his flair for the dramatic in my story.)

Below, you'll find my adaption of "The Johari Window" for Christians. The goal of our life, as believers, is to move out of the

Figure #2: The Johari Window

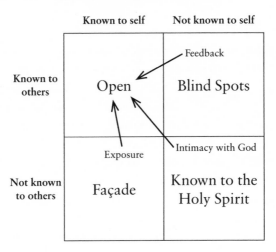

173

blind spot and façade quadrants and into the "open" area. That is the path of authenticity, of integration, of being *real*. In order to do that, we need three things, labeled with arrows.

In order for us to see and respond to the blind spots in our lives, we need loving feedback from others. This is the kind of encouragement and admonition Paul exhorts the church to practice in Romans 15:14: "I myself am convinced, my brothers and sisters, that you yourselves are full of goodness, filled with knowledge and competent to instruct one another." The Greek word rendered "instruct" here is *noutheteo*, a powerful verb that suggests the idea of gracious confrontation, based on the Word of God, which leads others to change.

For most of us, there are two uncomfortable dynamics to this reality. One, we don't want to be confronted, and two, most of us don't really want to *be* confronters. Avoiding blind spots is easier for everyone, right? Wrong! "If we keep patting each other on our broken backs," Beth Moore wisely pointed out, "how will they ever mend?"[11]

I challenge you to courageously ask one or two friends this question: "Is there anything in my life that you think I'm blind to?" I dare you! I am going to do it this week, and I'll let you know how it goes. Please share your story on my website, www .jandjclark.com.

Loving, God-honoring feedback (*noutheteo*) will help you come out of hiding. Exposure will as well. Most of us fear exposure even more than feedback. The word "exposure" connotes being caught unaware and having the ugliest parts of us dragged out for public view. That's not what I'm talking about here. I'm encouraging you to allow your weaknesses to be used for God's glory. I cannot tell you how many women have courageously shared with me their wounds after I willingly told them mine.

I have found tremendous freedom in owning my story and believe that you can too. In her wonderful book, *The Gifts of Imperfection*, Brené Brown observes, "Owning our story can be hard but not nearly as difficult as spending our lives running from it. Embracing our vulnerabilities is risky but not nearly as dangerous as giving up on love and belonging and joy—the experiences that make us the most vulnerable. Only when we are brave enough to explore the darkness will we discover the infinite power of our light."[12] Because Jesus is the Truth, authenticity brings his limitless power and unquenchable light into your life.

You earn greater respect, confidence, and freedom when you *press into* rather than run from exposure. This is where *being rather than seeming* becomes a reality. This week, ask God to show you someone with whom you can share part of your story, perhaps a part you've been hesitant to share with anyone before. If he reveals someone you're supposed to talk with, do so with courage. Trust his judgment and obey his promptings. Always keep in mind: it's the cracks in us that allow Jesus's light to shine through!

Finally, if you desire to come out of hiding, stop pretending with God. When you cultivate intimacy with him, the Holy Spirit will help you grow in authentic integration. He will take those parts of you that feel out of control and fearful and make them something absolutely beautiful. I know this because he has done and is *still*—at this very moment—doing it in me. The best way to come out of hiding with God is to practice the prayer of silence, and I'd like to turn our attention to that now.

Practicing the Prayer of Silence

Genesis 3 reveals what Adam and Eve did after sin entered the world by their choice: they *hid*. They hid, then they covered themselves, and then they blamed someone else for everything that went down. Sad to say, we've been doing the same ever since. Humans are creatures of constant evading, posturing, and shifting responsibility.

Nothing rips the charade of our pretense off like silence, and that's why most of us avoid it as vehemently as trying on bathing suits in public (dear God, isn't there a better way?!). In silence, we're alone with the raw ramblings of an untamed mind, a broken heart, or a troubled spirit. Sometimes it's all three boiling over inside us.

There's absolutely no escaping the truth that God values silence, however. Habakkuk 2:20 proclaims, "The Lord is in his holy temple; let all the earth be silent before him." Psalm 46:10 famously exhorts, "Be still, and know that I am God; I will be exalted among the nations, I will be exalted in the earth." And Zechariah 2:13 commands, "Be silent before the Lord, all humanity, for he is springing into action from his holy dwelling" (NLT). In the secret, silent places of our hearts, God springs into action.

If we refuse to practice silence, we are destined to lead noisy, crowded lives with little space for authenticity and intimacy with the Spirit. To be honest, some people want it that way. Faith can be rather intrusive, and silence reminds us of all the gunk hanging around in our mind and heart. When you get quiet and all your fears and unchecked desires come bubbling to the surface, it's unnerving to say the least. I'm in a period right now where I am sorely out of practice with silence. I've blamed it too long on being under deadline and having more things to do than twenty-four hours can hold. Ladies, that's true of your life and my life as long as we choose for it to be true. We don't have time to waste being noisy. If we want to be *real*, we have to do something different.

When I was young, my mom read me a beautiful little story called *The Velveteen Rabbit*. Perhaps you've read it too. In the end, the sweet stuffed bunny who becomes real is the one who's been loved so fiercely his fur is hugged off, and held so tightly during a battle with deadly illness that he has to go through a cleansing fire. To become real, you and I may have to have some fur loved off us. Some fire may need to purify us. But we will be freer and more beautiful than ever. Silence does this.

In silence, *stuff* rises to the surface. Thankfully, this need not be a source of fear but can become a source of strength for us; in silence, God introduces his power into our lives. Indeed, affirm *Beloved Dust* authors Jamin Goggin and Kyle Strobel, "Everything that comes out of our hearts in the presence of God is an invitation to be known by him. Whether it is fear, shame, pride, anxiety, or even lust, our call is to open those things before him and receive redemption as those who desperately need it."[13]

Encouraging you to practice silence is important, but I cannot give you a precise formula for what to do with the silence. That is up to God. I do urge you to start small and give yourself lots of grace. Try for two to five minutes if you're not used to practicing silence. It will feel plenty long! During this time, make your solitary goal that experience which Isaiah described, "You will keep in perfect peace those whose minds are steadfast, because they trust in you" (26:3). Give him all your attention and trust; receive his perfect peace. This will be challenge enough.

For some, sitting in silence feels "pointless"; *I'm not doing anything*, they lament. Not true! The prayer of silence simply shifts activity from the surface of your life to the deeper places of the spirit, places beneath even the threshold of your consciousness. Because silence requires you to surrender and opens you to God's work, it's not exactly easy. Jeanne Guyon wisely notes, "You must realize, dear reader, that the soul of man is naturally restless and turbulent. Your soul accomplishes very little even though it always appears busy." Thankfully, continues Guyon, practicing silence alters things. "When something is repeated over and over, it becomes a *habit*. This is true even of your soul. After much practice, your soul forms the *habit* of turning inward to God."[14]

As you become more comfortable with intimacy with God through silence, you may wish to set aside longer periods for silent waiting on him. There are some wonderful resources that give further instruction regarding silent prayer. I've listed a couple below. One form I enjoy practicing is called "wordless prayer."

In wordless prayer, we allow God to bring thoughts, emotions, and people to mind. We deliberately choose not to interrupt or attempt to control this process with words ("talking" to God about what comes up). Instead, we listen for what God might say to us as things "parade" past our attention. Simply looking at something in God's presence often enables me to understand it and let it go, if need be. In fact, the retreat at which I learned to practice wordless prayer used the phrase "look and let go" as an identifier for this form of Godward contemplation. Other times I sense something specific that God wants me to do about what he's brought to mind; perhaps it's conviction of sin or a change that he's asking me to make. Sometimes I hear nothing. That, too, is part of the process.

Whatever way your practice of silence takes shape, remember that, while there is no formula, there is always *him*. God is the purpose of practicing silence. The aim is not to get some dramatic revelation or even to know clearly what your next step of obedience is. The goal is always, ever, to have more of him. In looking at him, you will discover your true and beloved self.

～～～

Questions for Personal Reflection or Group Discussion:

1. How do you see "seeming rather than being" played out around you? What is one step you could take to *be* rather than *seem*?

2. Are you willing to do the two things recommended in this chapter: (1) Ask someone, "Is there anything in my life that you think I'm blind to?" and (2) authentically share your story with someone? Why or why not?

3. Is it easy or difficult for you to be silent? What do you sense when you're quiet before the Lord?

Recommended Reading:

- Barton, Ruth Haley. *Invitation to Solitude and Silence: Experiencing God's Transforming Presence*. Downers Grove, IL: InterVarsity Press, 2010.
- Brother Lawrence, *The Practice of the Presence of God*. An indispensable spiritual classic, written in the 1600s. Many editions are available.

{10}

Giving Your Life So That Others Might Live

True or false: my sexuality is something to celebrate.

True or false: my sexuality is part of the perfect image of God reflected in me.

True or false: my feminine sexuality brings life to the world and glory to God.

Do these questions strike you as odd?

Chances are, you haven't been asked them recently (or, more realistically, ever!). In fact, I'm willing to bet that most of us have spent far too little time thinking about sex.

Why? Because daydreaming about sex, watching romantic scenes, experimenting with sex, obsessing about having or not having it, being terrified of it, sensing shame because of it, and feeling the pleasure or pain of sexual expression are not the same as really *thinking* about sex.

But think about it we must.

Your sex life matters to God. Your sexuality was created to bring him glory. As a woman, you were uniquely designed to bring life into the world. And all of that is true regardless of whether you ever "do it" or not, whether you bear children biologically, whether you experience orgasm or horrific abuse.

Sex and life are inextricably connected. No human life comes into this world without engaging male and female sexuality, even if a sperm and egg are brought together in a laboratory. Those seeds of life still come from a man and a woman, God's perfectly ordained carriers of life.

Some of you may hate sex. Perhaps even seeing the word written turns your stomach. The only sexual expression you can imagine may be shameful, abusive, or frightening.

Others of you are dismissive. Sex is something you do—or would do—for someone else, but you scoff at the idea that your sexuality matters to God, let alone brings him glory. Some of you find sex a chore, and you're resigned to it because "it's an important part of marriage (but only for my husband)."

Still others of you, my friends, are consumed with sex. You may be obsessed with technique, drawn to fantasies you'd be ashamed to admit enjoying, or suffering from a life-debilitating addiction to pornography.

Some, though perhaps fewer of you, relish your sexuality. Maybe you're single and love being right where you're at. Others are wives and mothers who find joy in sexual expression. Tying sex, freedom, and life together is no stretch for you.

Perhaps you identify with different aspects of these groups. You may have been or may now be straddling one or more of these descriptions. Wherever you are, I hope that as we explore this topic, you'll courageously journey with me. We need to be brave to think about sex because it always involves far more than physical sensations. My hope is that this chapter will help you connect your sexuality with life: life-giving, life-enjoying, and life in Christ.

Note: Those of you who are single may be wondering whether you should skip this chapter. *I'm not having sex, so it's not really applicable to me*, you might be thinking. I invite you to consider this: you are a sexual being whether or not you ever have sex. Your sexuality is part of your identity for as long as you walk this earth, because you will never cease being a *woman*.[1] God's perfect plan included making you a woman, and he wants you to relish your femininity. Because he is Life, Jesus wants you to be part of life in this world, specifically as a woman. You and I give life or deal death with every word and action; we are constantly adding to the woundedness or partnering with God's redemptive work here on earth. Because Jesus is Life, you are called to give life whatever your circumstances.

With these thoughts in mind, let's turn our attention to how all women—single and married—can bring glory to God through life-giving.

Before We Begin . . .

This book is not an exegetical commentary. While I have attempted to share the contextual dynamics at play in Jesus's "I am" statements, and while studying the original languages in which the Bible was written as well as cross-references pertinent to Christ's claims has been essential in my writing, I don't consider myself a biblical scholar.

For this chapter, in particular, such a disclaimer is significant, as I am in no way asserting that Jesus was specifically talking about sexuality when he told his followers, "I am the Way, the Truth, and the Life." I hope that my introduction to chapters 8, 9, and 10 gave enough context and explanation to launch us into our study, but if you would like more commentary and exegesis on this passage (John 14:6), I have included some suggested resources in the endnotes.

However, because I believe so strongly that sexuality is a stumbling block for Christian women in their relationships to their own bodies, other people, and God himself, I didn't want to write a book on identity without exploring this topic. I also wanted to be absolutely faithful to the biblical text. That's why I want to make clear, right from the beginning of this chapter, that I am speaking particularly of *one* aspect of God's image in women: the capacity to give life because he is the Life.

Because Jesus is Life, we reflect his procreative character. Christ—as the Author of physical life and the Perfecter of spiritual life through sanctification on earth and eternal worship in heaven—imprints every human with the ability to give life. This is both true of our reproductive bodies and true of our spiritual calling to bear the fruit of kingdom work, especially making disciples.

Part of the reason infertility is such an agonizing struggle for those who suffer with it is because women innately *feel*—even if they never act on this sense and even if they are unable to conceive—that they were *meant* to bring life into the world. If you're currently in this position, my heart goes out to you. I didn't have a menstrual cycle for four years as a result of my eating disorder and spent a good deal of time worried that I wouldn't be able to have biological children. Though I was eventually able to conceive, I wasn't able to breast-feed well. I felt like a failure as a woman and a mom because even though I had the "equipment" to nurse, I could not force things to work (and believe me, my friend, I drank gallons of mother's milk tea, brought in the Boob Nazis—a.k.a. lactation consultants, and ate every "recommended" food to boost my milk production). Having that experience and going through the grief of not being able to give life to my kids through nursing gave me a glimmer—a tiny, tiny window—into what it might feel like to battle infertility. Wanting to give life is common to most women because Jesus created us to be life-givers.

To know that you have all the "plumbing" for pregnancy, but not be able to experience it, must be agonizing. I pray that you'll be able to read this chapter about sexuality and know that I write with you in mind, with your struggle close to my heart, and your desire to give life in my prayers to Jesus, the one and only Life-giver. He is not withholding from you or punishing you. His heart for you is good. It may take time for you to rediscover that, but please "press on to know the LORD" (Hos. 6:3 NASB). He *will* be found when you seek him, Jeremiah 29:13 promises.

Let's Talk about Sex . . .

If you were a teenager in the nineties, you may have unwittingly started singing the title of this section. A popular song during my high school days urged me to talk about sex—about all the good things and the bad things that may be. I complied, though I'm sure my arrogant adolescent self would have rejected the idea that I was obeying a stupid, teenybopper song.

Still, the reality was, I talked about sex with my friends . . . a lot. Way more than I hope my teenage daughters will talk about it with their peers (but, gulp, they probably will anyway). Natural curiosity about sex, mixed with cultural saturation in erotic innuendo, images, and idolatry leaves most Christian women with a head-splitting case of confusion.

As a young believer, my sex education basically boiled down to "just say no," but then I got married and I was instantaneously supposed to become an adventurous and willing partner for my husband. Did I miss the part of my marriage ceremony where I got bibbity-bobbity-booed into a sex kitten? Is that even what I'm supposed to be?

Growing up, there was little discussion in my Bible studies about delighting in holy sexuality. (I don't even remember hearing those terms connected until I had already been married several years.) While this has changed some in the intervening years, most of the conversations that I have with women—whether my married friends, the single gals I mentor, or those who sneak up to me after I give a talk on the subject—revolve around disappointment with or alienation from their own bodies, their sexual desire and pleasure, and the sense that sex should be something more than a five-and-a-half-minute act in the dark.

With the rise of widely celebrated erotic books, the mainstreaming of pornography, gender confusion, and the constant barrage of messages about our own sex life and the details of celebrities' doings, women are in a more complicated position than ever before. That's why it's essential that we understand sex within a biblical context. Sexuality was meant, on every level, for life: the enjoyment of life, the building of life, the passing on of life, and the eventual worship of God in eternity.

Sexuality—male and female—is a pre-fall design. In this way, there was "sex" in Eden, in the paradise God created. Men and women were given the mandate to "be fruitful and multiply" *before* they were cast out of Eden, and unless you want to argue that didn't include intercourse, we have to accept that God views sex as part of his very good, perfectly holy, and reflective-of-his-divine-character design.

Have you ever pondered the implications of the image God selected to describe his covenant relationship with his people? He chose a *marriage* to be the picture of Christ and his church (see Eph. 5:21–33). Intimacy with Jesus is supposed to be like intimacy between a beloved and a lover. Like it or not, sexuality—not strictly the act of sex, but the expression of masculinity and femininity in all its dynamics—is intended to help us understand God better.

No wonder the enemy wants to fill our minds and our bedrooms with smut! He wants to disconnect your sexuality from love, intimacy, holiness, and God-honoring worship. He'll do anything within his power to make you despise your sexuality, resign yourself to boring sexual expression in marriage, fixate your single life on "finding the one," or any number of other attacks. He'll introduce bitterness or addiction, fear or shame whenever and wherever he can. He prompts abusers to abuse, tainting sex with pain and terror. He prowls around, looking for women to devour.

Because Jesus is the Author of Life, gives us the capacity to give life, and commands us to do so, I believe a basic grasp of the following principles will help us embrace life-giving as God devised it. Some of these touch directly on sexual expression. Others relate more to sexuality as a whole (i.e., our feminine nature). We'll spend a bit of time looking at each of the following truths:

1. Life-giving is a lifestyle and a lifelong pursuit.
2. Love is the heart of life-giving.
3. God created women to be women, so seeking the kind of equality that "erases" gender is an affront to God's plan and therefore detrimental to femininity.
4. Since love is the heart of life-giving, any expression of sexuality devoid of love is a betrayal of God's perfect design.

A Lifelong Lifestyle

Regardless of whether we have many children or none, whether we're single, have long, happy marriages, or relationships that end in tragedy or betrayal, none of us can escape the reality that we give life or deal death with every word and deed. Each choice we make adds to the pain or pleasure of this world and our fellow sojourners on this planet. Many of the choices we *don't* make deliberately but default to anyway bring life or death to ourselves, those around us, and the created world. We'll look at this first on a broad and general level, identifying the struggles women face in using their words to give life to others. Toward the end of this section, we'll specifically apply the truths we learn to the way we talk about sexuality.

I am a big talker. I love talking; people even pay me to talk (with the expectation, stated or assumed, that I'll say something life-giving). Because I talk a lot, I know well what Proverbs 10:19 teaches: "When there are many words, transgression is unavoidable, but he who restrains his lips is wise" (NASB).

One profound way that *all* women can give life is by learning to watch our words. I love how the 1996 New Living Translation renders the second half of Proverbs 10:19: "Be sensible and turn off the flow!" Sometimes, to give life, we have to zip it!

If you want to give life, you can also set yourself apart as a woman who speaks life. Women are notoriously associated with gossip, backbiting, criticism, and nit-picking. The biblical epistles even name particular women in the ancient churches who were dealing death through their vicious words. God forbid we follow in their footsteps! Let's fight stereotypes by being women who speak life into a hurting world.

Here are a couple practical ways to start giving life through your words:

- If someone begins to tell you something slanderous, even if it's disguised as a prayer request, graciously stop them. For instance, next time a friend starts a conversation by saying, "I probably shouldn't tell you this . . . ," why not reply, "You're right! I have enough negative thoughts already. Thanks for sparing me any more."

- Deliberately choose to bless others, even when you don't feel like it. For women, many of our words actually go unsaid. We curse people under our breath or in the quiet corners of our imagination. This must end if we're to give life to others. When the bitter words toward someone else arise in your mind, stop and say—I find that out loud is sometimes the best way to really break a pattern of thought—"God, in the name of Your Son, Jesus, I bless _____." You don't have to tell God what to bless them for or with; he's God. He can figure out that part. You simply choose to give life by stopping venomous thoughts.

- Your words—both the spoken and unspoken ones—reveal what's in your heart, so fill your heart with good things. This is not my idea; it's directly from Scripture! Matthew 12:34b puts it plainly: "The mouth speaks what the heart is full of." If your heart is full of jealousy, anger, resentment, disapproval, and condemnation, it will come out in your words. In order to reflect Life to the world, we need to have hearts that overflow with life. This can only occur as we intentionally spend time filling our hearts with truth. You must *actively choose* what you allow into your heart. Defaulting to whatever is around you will not fill your heart with life, for this world is full of death in various forms. Instead, we must habitually choose to spend time with the Source of Life, that our hearts might be full of his love and truth.

Unlike some callings (including motherhood), which are limited to particular seasons of life, our calling as life-givers is a lifelong vocation. Women must choose, over and over, which lifestyle they will embrace: life-giving or death-dealing. This decision should impact what we say about, well, *everything*. The vast majority of us, if consciously aware of the choice, would opt to give life rather than add to the pain of the world. The trouble is, our vicious and manipulative enemy presents death-dealing lifestyles of judgment, criticism, and discontent as acceptable and perhaps even necessary.

"If you don't tell him there's something wrong with what he's doing, who will?!" leads women to nagging and criticizing those around them. The accuser suggests a thought—"She's just getting what she deserves"—and it ends in gossip and judgmentalism. Or the idea, "God knows that I'll be better able, once I . . . or once He gives me . . ." gradually turns into bitter dissatisfaction with the life we've been given.

Here's the direct application to our role as women: how we speak about femininity, sexuality, and sexual expression adds to the hurt or hope in the world. There is plenty of "talk" about sex, but precious few women reflect Life through the way they talk about sexuality or being a woman. Most of us complain and lament about the "trials" of womanhood—from periods and PMS to pregnancies and perimenopause—but when was the last time you and a group of girlfriends spent time thanking God for the unique gift of your feminine nature and body? If never, I dare you to start making a list of the specific blessings of being a woman and share it with someone close to you (your daughter, mom, sister, or best friend perhaps). We can and should celebrate our God-ordained design as women.

How you talk about sex also impacts how much life is in this world. Don't scoff at this idea; it's true! I hear so many married women complaining about "how much my husband wants it," asking with frustration, "Why does sex matter that much?" I hear single women lamenting about not being able to find a guy to date who *isn't* affected in some way by pornography. This is an incredibly serious problem; perhaps we should spend more time praying for rather than verbally rehearsing the sins of our brothers. I just yesterday read a book that details the horrific presence of sexual assault on college campuses. My heart broke as I read the story of a young woman who was told, while her assailant stole her virginity, "Why are you crying? It's just sex; it doesn't matter. It's nothing."

How we talk and think about sex is far from nothing; it's a *crucial* thing, because sex and life-giving were *always* intended to begin and end with love.

The Heart of Life-Giving

The antithesis of love isn't always hate. Indeed, for many of us, the force that most opposes our call as life-givers is not contempt, but rather selfishness. Being a life-giver is a lifelong and often laborious lifestyle. It ain't easy being a woman, and it's especially hard for a woman committed to reflecting Life to the world; her every movement toward love and sacrifice will be opposed by an enemy who wants to use her as a death dealer!

As the ultimate life-giver, Jesus revealed that giving life involves suffering and death. As we discussed with regard to Christ's claim, "I am the resurrection and the life," Jesus *had* to die to bring us life. In a similar manner, we *must* die to the selfish desires that keep us from giving life if we are to fulfill our calling as women. Thankfully, the book of 1 Timothy provides some helpful guidance for those of us who want to make love central to our life-giving.

The apostle Paul writes, "But women will be saved through childbearing—if they continue in faith, love and holiness with propriety" (1 Tim. 2:15). This is an extremely perplexing verse upon first glance. What in the world does this mean? Women will be "saved" through childbearing?[2]

Because of complementary passages later in 1 Timothy (specifically 4:16), we know that this reference to "salvation" is not about the legal transaction of justification from sin, which was secured *only* and *absolutely* by Jesus on the cross. Instead, 1 Timothy 2:15's reference to "be[ing] saved" concerns the ongoing process of sanctification by which we are made more like Jesus and better prepared to worship him for eternity in heaven.

Women are made more like Christ by giving life. For many women, this follows a common path of bearing children physically; this, by matter of course, includes the sanctity of sexual intercourse for procreation. For other women, the path of sanctification involves surrendering that capacity in order to bring life to the world in different ways. Paul writes of this in 1 Corinthians 7, a passage which details the high value God places on singlehood; Jesus honors those who choose to remain unattached so that they can focus more intently on him (see vv. 34–35, in particular).

In whichever way God chooses to sanctify you—whether as a married or single woman—the *means* of life-giving is the same: "continue in faith and love and sanctity with self-restraint" (1 Tim. 2:15 NASB).

Faith in God allows us to stop relying on ourselves and trust in him to renew us. When we are continually refreshed by God and confident in his loving care, we can give life to others. Fear and discontentment are cast out by this perfect love.

Love is the perfect antidote for selfishness, which is the greatest obstacle to life-giving. When John the Baptist proclaimed Jesus "must become greater; I must become less" (John 3:30), he spoke this fundamental truth: *we cannot become who we were designed to be if we seek our own increase*. It must always and only be Jesus that we desire to glorify. When our eyes are fixed on him in love, his grace and compassion flow through us to others. This brings more of Jesus—the Life—to the world. When our eyes are fixed on our own prerogatives, passions, and pleasure, we deal death to others and ourselves.

Sanctity involves being set apart. As a woman, God set you apart for womanhood. This isn't up for debate. His purpose for you includes embracing and glorifying him through your femininity. Being set apart in this way is a gift, and one to be taken seriously, not mocked or dismissed or theologized away. Being set aside as a life-giver means sanctifying our time and actions for giving life. This may include surrendering your plans for how *you* would like to give life. You may have wanted children from the time you were playing with dolls. If that is not God's plan for you, will you still choose to reflect Life to the world in the ways he does ordain? You may not feel like having sex as often as your husband. Are there times when you can unselfishly give life by being a willing lover?

On the other hand, you may feel rejected by your husband or undesirable to him. Sex has become a constant reminder of your "not good enoughness," and that part of your marriage feels more like experiencing repeated death than giving life. Perhaps the truth of your belovedness in Christ feels weak compared to the heartache you bear. I encourage you to renounce the lie that you are unwanted or unworthy. The enemy wants you to believe that; your husband may unwittingly—or maliciously—be perpetuating that lie, but God will never reject, abandon, or dismiss you. He cherishes every piece of you. Align yourself with truth instead and boldly, lovingly confront the issues in your marriage. Pursue counseling for yourself; pray fervently that your husband would be convicted and healed; address specific problems, and do not allow lies to steal your confidence. You *are* accepted. You *are* chosen. You *are* beloved, and that will *never* change. Living in truth gives you the power to bring life to others and experience life yourself.

Some of you fear embracing your feminine sexuality. Perhaps past abuse or scornful and shameful memories have poisoned your ability to delight in holy sexuality. If so, I encourage you with all my heart to pursue counseling with a trusted counselor or clinician. These issues will not sort themselves out, and your sexuality is a major part of who you are. Not having sex, ignoring the messages you've heard or absorbed in the past, or looking down on sex won't solve this. There is hope, there is *life*, in finding peace with your womanhood. You were sanctified—set apart—as a woman, and God intends for you to experience redemption, the restoration of wholeness as a woman.

The final component of life-giving mentioned by Paul in 1 Timothy 2:15 is *self-restraint*. Self-control, a fruit of the Holy Spirit in our life, helps us in two ways. It enables us to (1) restrain urges to do what is outside God's perfect plan for us, and (2) find renewed energy when we're harried, tired, and depressed. Because we're life-givers marooned in a fallen world, we're continuously threatened with strain, drain, and dryness. Only in coming to Jesus, the Source of Life, do we find the strength to love rather than live selfishly, to sanctify ourselves for his purposes, and to say no to the sin that so easily entangles.

Both married and single women must exert constant vigilance with regard to their sexual purity. If you believe the need for purity ends when someone puts a ring on your fourth finger, think again! Married women must guard their sexual thoughts and desires every bit as fiercely as single women. That's why it's terribly dangerous for women to unrestrainedly watch provocative TV and films or read titillating books. Even seemingly innocuous novels written by people of faith may spark *in you* lustful fantasy. This happened to me! I got so engrossed in a series of Christian romance novels that I began daydreaming about one of the main characters. That's not healthy for my marriage or femininity, regardless if it's a "Christian" book or a fictional character.

I'm so grateful that I don't have to decide what *you* should and should not read, watch, or think. It's hard enough figuring out my own stuff. The Holy Spirit is responsible for you, and I entrust you to his wonderful care. I do encourage you, however, not to quiet his voice with justifications and rationalizations. Keep guard over your mind and heart, that you might be a faithful, loving, holy, and self-controlled life-giver.

The Right Kind of Equal

My sophomore year of college, I went out on a date with an intelligent, kind guy. I was looking forward to the date, but it ended up being totally bizarre. I'm not sure if he was trying to impress me with "progressive thinking," but he spent the whole time telling me how gender was a sociological construction and equality between the sexes could never happen if we perpetuated "myths" about masculinity and femininity. "We have to get rid of that whole idea so true equality can emerge." I kind of smiled and "hmm"ed, but inside I was thinking, *If there's no difference between the sexes, why in the world are we on this date?*

On the whole, humans see differences mostly in terms of value; because of this, "different" usually implies a comparison between better and worse. This is not, however, the way God views human sexuality. In God's perfect design, for two things to be equal in value, they don't have to be equal in nature. The primary distinction that separates us from our male counterparts—our feminine sexuality—has nothing to do with *value*; it does, however, have to do with *nature*.[3]

It's incredibly important for me and for anyone who desires equality for women to steer clear of the kind of egalitarianism that makes "equality" dependent on sameness. Sadly, I believe this is part of the sexual and gender confusion we find running rampant in modern culture.

For some of you, you wonder why I'd include this section at all; you've never wondered about this. Great! Others of you know exactly why I addressed this; messages about equality have left some of us bereft. What do women in this crazy, confused culture do with the evident distinctions between them and their male counterparts? Do we dismiss them, ignore them, try to overcome them with empowerment and liberation? Or is there, perhaps, a better way? A way that celebrates equality *and* difference, both part of God's perfect design. If we wish to enjoy our femininity and bring glory to God through our sexuality, our path is upholding, not betraying God's design for life.

Doing That Very Thing

As we've already noted, love is the very heart of life-giving, central both in motivation and action. Because of this, any expression of sexuality devoid of Christlike love is a betrayal of God's perfect design. Let's look at this in terms of two distinct stages of life: singlehood and marriage.

For my single friends, I offer an invitation to reject unhealthy fantasizing about what a "perfect" relationship should be. When I was single, I spent a lot of time wondering whether I'd get married, when I would if I did, what my life would be like in the future (this included thoughts about sex, most of which amounted to wanting to reenact particularly wonderful kiss scenes from my favorite chick flicks), and so on. Interestingly enough, I spent zero time thinking about the sacrifices that love might require of me, the despair I might feel when marriage didn't equal feeling perpetually loved, and the deliberate resolve love would necessitate. In short, I fantasized about my personal fulfillment/happiness and ignored the truth that life-giving costs a great deal.

Please understand me; I'm not encouraging you to dwell inordinately on these other, less immediately appealing aspects of love. That will only leave you in a similar predicament: thinking mostly about yourself. Instead, I invite you to practice life-giving by first focusing on Life himself—Jesus—and then loving those around you. Give life to others in the unique ways in which Jesus, the Life, created you to do. We mostly bring life to the world through the talents, abilities, and spiritual gifts God grants. Use all of those to give life to others! Many women, though not all, find that nurturing comes naturally to them; celebrate that feminine expression. Don't consider it a sign of weakness or so stereotypical that it should be suppressed. We give life when we focus on what is, rather than what we think should be. This brings glory to God.

For you married sisters out there: if you view sex mostly as an obligation that you resign yourself to now and then, I challenge you to consider where love fits into that equation. There have been times in my marriage when I've been frustrated by how *complicated* sex is. I had no idea that it took so much work to stay on the same page, to love one another well, to avoid the temptations to shut down love when I'm wounded. I recall one night when I felt particularly hurt by Jeramy; I knew I couldn't just stop having sex altogether, so I deliberately decided, "Well then, he can have my body, but he can't have my heart." *This* has been, perhaps, the greatest temptation of my sex life—to separate it from love.

My dear, married friends, having a healthy outlook on sex and a fulfilling sex life is neither simple nor swift. Because of this, we often lose heart; resignation may threaten to set in. "The new cultural belief that everything should be fun, fast, and easy is inconsistent with hopeful thinking. It also sets us up for hopelessness. When we experience something that is difficult and requires significant time and effort, we are quick to think, *This is supposed to be easy; it's not worth the effort. This should be easier . . .* or, I would add, *This is only hard and slow because my husband expects too much.*[4]

I'll be blunt: this must not continue! We cannot give in to this way of thinking. Our sex lives matter to God because they are part of his design for *love* and *life-giving*. When you give part of your life so that someone else can live more fully and more truly, you honor Jesus, the creator of love and life. Sex can be part of this. Together, let's choose to give of our love so that others might live.

Practicing the Prayers of Renewal and Relinquishment

Biologically speaking, life is neither perpetual nor independent; in order for something to continue living, it must derive sustenance from its environment. The moment a being ceases to receive necessary support from its surroundings, life terminates.

The spiritual parallel is profound. We can neither live ourselves, nor give life to others, if we are not continually renewed with life and love from God. The life he offers us—the abundant, eternal life we've discussed in this book—is transmitted to us *not* in a once-and-for-all-time transaction but rather in a *continuous* outpouring as we remain close to Jesus. His vitality, his vigor, his views become ours over time and through constant communion.[5]

The last time you got on an airplane, you heard the flight attendant describe what to do in the "unlikely event of a drop in cabin pressure": when the oxygen masks drop, put your own on before helping anyone else (even your infant child!). In a similar way, we *cannot*—it simply is not possible—to give life without being connected to Life himself.

One of the greatest secrets to a life of peace and patience is that it doesn't happen overnight. Accept his grace to breathe and grow and be transformed. This *will* happen as you spend time with Jesus, being renewed by and relinquishing yourself to him.

To practice the prayer of renewal, try taking a passage of Scripture that you find particularly comforting and beautiful. Next, imagine yourself in it. I love Psalm 23 for this. To deliberately picture myself beside still waters and at the table God has set before me, anointed with his oil of gladness, is renewing for me. Perhaps you like the passage in Isaiah 40 about soaring on wings like eagles (vv. 28–31). Maybe you love the words of Song of Solomon 6:3: "I am my beloved's and my beloved is mine." Use these!

Seek out other passages and meditate on them by prayerfully picturing yourself held in the arms of your loving heavenly Father (Deut. 33:27), gently led by a kind shepherd (Isa. 40:11), or at peace with God's protection and truth (Psalm 62). This practice will renew your spirit and give you strength to be a life-giver, as will practicing the prayer of relinquishment.

This prayer can also be called the prayer of surrender. I find it particularly helpful with regard to life-giving, as so much of love involves sacrifice and a laying down of my agenda and desires. Jesus's prayer in the Garden of Gethsemane is our perfect model here: "Not my will, but yours be done" (Luke 22:42).

One of my favorite novelists, Jan Karon, describes "Thy will be done" as "the prayer that never fails."[6] How true! When we relinquish our will and align ourselves with his, it *never fails*.

Are there areas of your life you need to relinquish? I don't even know why I phrased that as a question; I *know* there are areas of my life and yours that need to be surrendered to the Lord's control. Let us never forget that he alone is the blessed controller of all things (1 Tim. 6:15). Not only is he in control; he's *good* at being in control. When we relinquish ourselves to him in prayer, we join the side of victory! There is no risk in relinquishing yourself to God's care.

If you are a single woman, perhaps you feel called to relinquish your desires or plans for marriage. Whether God fulfills your dreams or not, surrendering your hopes aligns you with peace and his perfect plan. If you are a married woman and perhaps a mother, too, your prayer of relinquishment may involve letting go of what you pictured life and life-giving would be like.

Practice the prayer of surrender with me, right now: *Lord Jesus, not my will, but yours be done.* Repeat as often as necessary (for me, this is a lot!).

As you practice the prayers of renewal and relinquishment, I pray that you find great strength to be who God created you to be—a woman who brings him great glory!

~~~~

Questions for Personal Reflection or Group Discussion:

1. Do you believe that your feminine sexuality brings life to the world? Why or why not?

2. How do your words bring life or deal death to those around you? Do the ways you talk about being a woman and sex bring life to the world? What change(s) would you like to make?

3. What passage(s) would you like to use for the prayer of renewal, described on page 198?

Recommended Reading:

- Chandler, Matt. *The Mingling of Souls: God's Design for Love, Marriage, Sex, and Redemption.* Colorado Springs: David C. Cook, 2015.

- Pintus, Lorraine, and Linda Dillow. *Intimate Issues: Twenty-One Questions Christian Women Ask about Sex.* Colorado Springs: WaterBrook Press, 2009.

{11}

So Much More To Life Than This

One unsuspecting day in small-town Texas, the unthinkable occurred. Over two hundred children lost their lives in a blaze that consumed an elementary school faster than firefighters could extinguish it. Few families escaped from the tragedy unscathed; sons and daughters, nieces and nephews, as well as adult friends and colleagues lost their lives in a matter of minutes.

The town resolved to rebuild the school with state-of-the-art fire safety equipment. This included a highly advanced sprinkler system, which reputedly could detect and end a fire like that which had destroyed so much. Prior to the grand reopening of the elementary school, student survivors took townspeople on tours of the new buildings, showing off the safety features. Though the grief of loss was still fresh, a spirit of hopefulness pervaded the community.

Some years later, when population growth necessitated an addition to the school, a shocking discovery rocked the town. The cutting-edge sprinklers, the emergency equipment that had given so many families confidence to send their surviving children back to school, had never been connected to an external water source.

Despite its technological excellence, the system could never have worked, let alone saved lives. Connection was central to its purpose and effectiveness. The one thing that really mattered—its power to protect—depended on an outside supply, a resource the sprinklers could neither provide nor maintain on their own; without that, the entire system was useless.[1]

The When, Where, and Why

Connection is central to my purpose and effectiveness too. The same is true for you. Without constant reliance on a strength and peace, love and grace greater than ourselves, we are like that ill-fated sprinkler system: huge potential, zero power.

Jesus knew this well, so he spoke openly of his own intimate relationship with the heavenly Father, modeled communion with him in the Spirit, and urged his disciples to cultivate the same. Perhaps his most famous words on this theme can be found in John 15. They are also Christ's final "I am" statement:

> I am the vine, you are the branches. If you remain in me and I in you, you will bear much fruit; apart from me you can do nothing. (John 15:5)

This small but mighty verse forms part of a longer passage[2] that touches on our relationship with God, our purpose in this life, and the glory that awaits us in the next. It's part of his "Farewell Discourse," the last words Jesus chose to share with his beloved disciples before his betrayal, crucifixion, and triumphant resurrection. Safe to say, he really wanted them—and he really wants us—to remember this truth: if you stay close to me, you will have meaning and fulfillment; separated from me, there is only emptiness. Connection is key to purpose and effectiveness.

The focal word of John 15 is the Greek term *menó* (μένω), rendered "remain" or "abide" by our English translations. Jesus uses this term, in its various grammatical constructions, no less than fifteen times in the first ten verses of John 15. Since repeating something one or two times is a way to emphasize importance, fifteen repetitions might be the biblical equivalent of a flashing neon sign, complete with giant exclamation point.

If you grew up in the church or have heard a sermon on the book of John, chances are this idea of "abiding" isn't entirely new to you. If you're anything like me, however, you might have wondered, *What does that really mean? How exactly do I do that?*

For many years, I knew that Jesus invited me to be connected with him, to remain in him. I knew cognitively—I had memorized the verse, after all—that I could do nothing apart from Christ (John 15:5). Still, I often lived as if what Jesus really meant was "You can do most of life on your own, but when you need help or get stuck, then pray and I'll give you the added strength you need." Sad to say, I lived as if God acted more like a boost in my power smoothie than the source of the whole works.

The truth is, Jesus doesn't say "apart from me you're handicapped and need assistance" or "separate from me you're weakened and need something for enhanced performance." The Greek word he chose is ου: *no*-thing, nada, the empty set. This rubs my Western-minded, American-proud independence the wrong way. I don't like considering myself unable, limited, entirely dependent. This is, however, precisely what Jesus invites me to embrace. The promise attached: when I live this truth (not merely assent to it or parrot it in spiritual conversations, but actually *live* it), then I will "bear much fruit." Could part of the reason many Christian women don't abide in Christ be because they don't really see "bearing fruit" as something exciting or desirable?

True confession: I'm not especially horticultural. In fact, I'm pretty sure I have a black thumb rather than a green one; plants seem either terrified of me or defiantly determined to die despite my best intentions. Bearing fruit may not communicate to my more-than-agriculturally-challenged self, but every woman—myself included—longs to have a *fruitful* life, a phrase we associate with fulfillment and meaning. Not one of us, given an overt choice, would opt for a life devoid of purpose, an unrewarding existence, a sense of worthlessness. We yearn to know why and for what we were made, and we want to live into that well. This search drives both the rapture and the restlessness of our days. Some of us feel that we're perpetually failing at this; others of us have quenched this longing because it seems too difficult or we fear failure. Few of us lean into a life of fruitfulness, unashamed and unafraid.

Jesus makes clear, however, that fruitfulness—meaning, purpose, joy, and peace—is what you and I were created to enjoy. Sin broke the relationship of intimate communion our heavenly Father originally designed us to enjoy, but Christ's death in our stead redeems the years and the yearnings sin has twisted. Since the key to this is connection—or abiding—let's look at what abiding is, what it entails, and where it leads us.

Gripping Your Bible Tightly

As is so often the case in life, figuring out what abiding *isn't* proves every bit as important as determining what it is. Abiding is *not* a matter of willpower. And guess what, dear one? That is *very good news!*

Jesus, our perfect example of abiding in the Father, did not white-knuckle his way through betrayal, loss, and trial. He didn't grit his teeth, dig down deep, and plow through like some sort of divine ninja warrior. In many ways, the American Dream—pulling oneself up from the ashes of defeat, overcoming seemingly insurmountable odds, and being able to say, with pride, "Look where I came from!"—is actually antithetical to the Christian message: on our own, we can do *nothing.*

Tragically, we often live as if our relationship with Jesus depends on *our own ability* to keep it going; in other words, on our willpower. Whether consciously or not, many of us have bought into the myth that if we try just a little bit harder, apply the right combination of spiritual practices (Bible study, prayer, service, etc.), and stick to them like glue, then we'll get beyond our struggles with sin, our sense that there's got to be more to life than this, our waiting for the weekend or the next vacation or pay raise or whatever. How did we come to believe that it's *our* personal commitment that leads to growth and transformation? It's insanity![3]

During college, I was involved with a parachurch organization that focused heavily on disciplined discipleship. Daily devotionals were not merely suggested; it was implied that without them, I could not grow. Combined with my already highly driven, perfectionistic temperament, this solidified a tacit assumption in my heart and mind: if I *don't* do this, I've failed; if I *do* accomplish this, I've succeeded. Unfortunately, believing this made my "quiet time" with Christ one more thing that I could do—and measure as—"right" or "wrong." I was very committed to the practices of Bible study, prayer, etc., but I had little true *communion* with Jesus. I doubt I would've been able to define what that even was! I did lots of Christian things and could tell you lots of very correct Christian answers, but I was restless inside. There had to be something more than this! My heart ached for connection, but I couldn't *make* that happen.

Abiding is not about willpower. That's not to say that choice plays no role in abiding; it's a key component! Neither you nor I will naturally remain in Christ; the decision to drift away or remain in him will confront us *every day* of our earthly life. That said, even our capacity to commit to connection with Jesus is dependent on the grace of the Holy Spirit. As Philippians 2:13 reveals, "It is God who works in you to will and to act in order to fulfill his good purpose." You and I don't even have the will—the desire or the resolve—to act and fulfill our purpose; that, too, comes from God! This should come as a relief to you, my sister. Figuring life out, making it work . . . you don't have to scramble to get it all together. It doesn't come down to you!

Thanks be to God, abiding never depends on my ability to tenaciously cling to Jesus. While we often and rightly speak of the power of God "in us," and the presence of the Holy Spirit within, we sometimes neglect the truth that—over and over again—the Bible describes us as *in Christ*. Our most essential position of identity is that we are hidden in Christ, not off on our own with him giving us a boost every now and then (see Colossians 3:3).

If you see abiding as one more thing you have to do, stay on top of, and/or succeed at, it's no stretch of the imagination to think you won't find it particularly exciting or desirable. Indeed, far too many Christians have resigned themselves to a false belief: I guess abiding isn't for me; I've tried it, but I'm just not very good at it. It must be for the superspiritual, those Christians who successfully have daily devotions, memorize Scripture, etc.

Is this our definition of "success" in the life of faith? If so, abiding will *seem* illusive. I say seem because this is neither the truth of our situation, nor of the nature of remaining in Jesus.

Think of the picture Christ uses in John 15 to illustrate abiding. Are branches throughout the world berating themselves for not being able to hold on to the vine better or produce more fruit? No! The relationship between a vine and healthy branches, laden with fruit, is *organic* (i.e., naturally occurring).

Despite the availability of countless books, posts, podcasts, and sermons on *being* as opposed to *doing*, many Western Christians are still caught up in a quasi-abiding that looks more like a repackaging of the American Dream—try harder, do better, and ultimately overcome—than a natural, organic communion with Christ.

Perhaps abiding seems difficult because if we want to truly experience communion with Jesus, we must slow down—stop, even—and most of us are very slow (irony intended) to sign up for that. We'd rather add one more spiritual practice (a class at church, a faith-based book club, meeting with a mentor) than sit alone, abiding. I think a lot of us have built our busy lives around a fear we don't even recognize; we're afraid of what we might find if we stop long enough to make ourselves at home in Christ. May it not be so for you or I, my friend!

For the Joy

My own movement away from doing things for Jesus and toward remaining close to him didn't happen happily. Instead, it's been the greatest trials of my life that have propelled me into genuine communion with Christ. When I literally could do *nothing* because I was catatonic with depression (this is not an exaggeration) or curled up in a fetal position with the agony of another debilitating headache, it became clear: abiding comes down to saying yes to Jesus, remaining in him, whether in paucity or plenty, pain or pleasure.

Wish I could tell you differently, but pain has been God's oft-appointed pathway to peace in my life, and let's just say that I'm not alone on that front. Indeed, Jesus's final "I am" statement in John 15 directly connects suffering, abiding, and fruitfulness: "I am the true vine, and my Father is the gardener. He cuts off every branch in me that bears no fruit, while every branch that does bear fruit he prunes so that it will be even more fruitful" (vv. 1–2).

A couple very happy truths arise from reading this passage carefully. One involves those whom Jesus describes as "bearing no fruit." While various translations render the Greek word, *airo*, as "taken away" or "cut off," this verb means "lifted up" in other contexts (Luke 17:13, John 11:41, Acts 4:24, and Rev. 10:5). For this reason, some modern commentators, including the eminently wise A. W. Pink, believe that a better English rendering would be "my Father *lifts up* or *repositions* every branch that is not bearing fruit."[4] Jesus never disqualifies his beloved ones from a life of future fruitfulness by cutting them off from himself entirely.

Jesus says that not bearing fruit is *like*—not is—being a withered, useless branch that one would toss on the fire (see John 15:6). Comparison is at play here, not equation. Our Lord lifts up and strengthens those who are not fulfilling their potential in him, and we can gratefully praise him for that, for all of us have been (or will be at some point) in that situation. Repositioning may be painful, but it will always be purposeful.

The second happy truth is closely related: pruning, too, is *never* pointless. In God's hands, your pain will never be wasted. I'm venturing to guess that most of you—women who've deliberately chosen to read a book like this—won't find this idea shocking, so I won't retread the ground that you likely know, that blessings often take the form of rain- or teardrops, that blessedness sometimes means bowing in surrender rather than triumphing over, and that beauty really does come from some ashes. I hope and pray you are living into these truths.

Right now, I'd like to encourage you to focus on suffering from a different angle. The book of Hebrews tells us that Jesus, for the *joy* set before him, endured the cross and scorned its shame (see 12:2). We endure the crosses of our own lives—the heartache, the hopelessness—and scorn the shame of loss and brokenness for the joy set before us too. We are made for a glory beyond that which we can imagine. Our pain is not only a pathway to peace; it's also a pathway to splendor.

C. S. Lewis penned one of the most beautiful articulations of this I've come across. In *Mere Christianity*, he writes,

> Imagine yourself as a living house. God comes in to rebuild that house. At first, perhaps, you can understand what He is doing. He is getting the drains right and stopping the leaks in the roof and so on; you knew that those jobs needed doing and so you are not surprised. But presently He starts knocking the house about in a

208

way that hurts abominably and does not seem to make any sense. What on earth is He up to? The explanation is that He is building quite a different house from the one you thought of—throwing out a new wing here, putting on an extra floor there, running up towers, making courtyards. You thought you were being made into a decent little cottage: but *He is building a palace*. He intends to come and live in it Himself.[5]

Jesus is the true vine, and our heavenly Father the Gardener who "chose you and appointed you so that you might go and bear fruit—fruit that will last" (John 15:16). Pruning is part of this process, but the end result is *fruit that will last*—a palace of his own making, not just a functional cottage that serves its purpose, but a place of beauty, careful design, and glorious magnificence.

You were made to share in glory! Your promised end is extravagant because your Father in heaven is transforming you into a palatial temple, God's very own dwelling place. We long for more in this life because we were created for shared majesty with the lover of our souls.[6]

Because of this, pruning and the pain it yields is not only far from pointless, it actually produces in us more than pure pleasure could. God wrote this truth into the life cycle of every plant so that we could see it at work; nature reminds us that we *must* be pruned to maximize fruitfulness.

I began with two happy truths about pruning: it's not pointless and it's for *joy* and *eternal glory* that we endure it. There are harder truths as well. One of the most challenging for me: pruning—both horticulturally and spiritually speaking—involves more than simply cutting away what is dead and useless. To prune well, a gardener must sometimes cut away living branches, ones that are already bearing fruit! Part of me revolts against this even as I write it. It seems cruel and unnecessary. I "get" trimming back those areas of our lives that are withered and worn, but why prune something that's alive and seemingly successful?

One reason is because laden branches often become too heavy. We have limits, even limits on how many "good" and "godly" things we can do. We cannot sustain the weight of carrying everything, nor did God ever intend us to do so. Sometimes our heavenly Father has to lovingly prune back branches that appear healthy and productive to us because he can see that the weight will eventually become too much. We don't have the eyes of eternity; most of us don't assess or respect our limits well. Praise be to God, Jesus does! He knows just how much weight we can bear and adjusts our load accordingly.

Another reason that living branches may need pruning is that Jesus's desire for us is maximum *fruitfulness*, not simply fruit production. Fruitfulness implies lavish abundance, the kind of "life to the limit" that John 10:10 describes. Our Father in heaven prunes even living branches because life is not ultimately about our "fruit production," it's about his grace overflowing in us.

Jesus doesn't need you to bear fruit. He can actually hack this whole sovereign-over-the-universe thing without you (no offense). Our life has always and ever been intended to point to what Christ is doing—preparing us for his glory, purifying us on the deepest levels, and implanting more of himself at the same time, all for the pleasure of our heavenly Father.

If your goal is simply to produce fruit, your sights are set too low. Fruit is an *outcome*, but it's never meant to be the end; fruitfulness is about God's ultimate glory! Fruit bearing happens naturally (think "organically"), as you focus on Jesus. This includes allowing the suffering in your life to mold and shape you, rather than fighting it, kicking and screaming, or trying to bury it beneath lots of good works, Christian books, sermons, and activities. Perhaps it's time to get your eyes off the fruit and the pruning and ask Jesus to show you the joy for which he's doing it all: his glory, the splendor that he longs and plans to share with you (with *you*!) in eternity. Only this vision can get us through the pain of pruning and palace building.

My Aha Moment

I can't recall when it happened, but at some point when I was studying suffering, I came across a description of the fruit pain produces in us. It is, of course, the fruit of the Spirit: love, joy, peace, patience, kindness, goodness, faithfulness, gentleness, and self-control (Gal. 5:22–23). This was no radical revelation. Then came a moment so—for lack of a better word—*momentous*, that I'm shocked I can't remember the particulars of how I first heard this. Here's the truth that astounded me: *Fruit takes time to ripen.*

Horticulturally speaking, there are no organic shortcuts to ripening fruit. My husband adores bananas, so he planted a banana tree in our backyard (bless his banana-lovin' heart). It took two whole years to bear fruit. Two years of waiting and watching and anticipating. And the bananas that eventually grew are brilliant; perhaps they're tastier because we eagerly expected them and rejoiced as they grew and colored and became ready to savor. Still, ripening happened *slowly*.

Spiritual fruit takes time to ripen too. We live in such an instant society, in a world where we think waiting is an obstacle to be overcome, not part of the divine process. We have somehow gotten it into our Western Christian minds that *God himself* wants us to produce fruit spontaneously, without patient trust. Most growth is slow, however, and many of us automatically equate slow with negative. If we produced fruit faster, we believe, we'd be able to do more for the kingdom and then God would . . .

What? Would God accomplish more if you and I were more efficient and more mature? Is he unable to achieve what he plans unless our spiritual fruit ripens fast and furiously? Is it up to you? Have you somehow aligned yourself with the false belief that God will love you more if you produce good fruit and, by extension, love you less if you're not doing "enough"? What is enough, anyway?

Love, joy, peace, patience, kindness, goodness, faithfulness, gentleness, and self-control. Do we actually expect these things to grow without some pressure and strain and *time*? Fruit needs time to ripen, but we're so busy trying to produce well that we don't embrace the process of slow growth.

Even writing that out, I get a bitter taste in my mouth at the words "process" and "slow." How sad that I've allowed the pressure of accomplishing and achieving to steal the joy set before me, the joy of watching and waiting and anticipating the fruit that *he* is ripening. Our family did it with the bananas; why not with spiritual fruit?

Maybe it's because we had been told that the fruit on our banana tree would take about two years to grow. We set our expectations accordingly. Perhaps if we actually believed and leaned into the truth that our spiritual growth will take time, we could slow down long enough to hear God's voice in the midst of the pruning, to trust his wise hands as the branches that have become too heavy for us are cut away, to grieve the losses that suffering inevitably brings, to eagerly expect his glory to shine through as we become more and more the splendorous palaces in which he dwells. All of this takes *time*, dear friend, and all of it happens when we abide. The fruit that then grows and ripens within will last. It will endure. I know this is what you ultimately desire; this is the significance we all crave. Sometimes it just plain *hurts*.

Suffering allows the true beliefs of your heart to surface. Part of the reason we want to avoid suffering is that to see ourselves as we truly are—still so afraid or selfish, still so caught up in the things of earth—is sometimes more painful than the trial itself. For most of us, the belief that we should be farther along in our spiritual life weighs on our souls. Because we assume that we're not where we "should be by now," we turn back to the kind of façades that we explored in chapter 9.

Pruning rips back the pretenses of our lives and exposes not only our true beliefs but also our true desires. If we have set our sights on anything less than God's glory—even good things like having a happy Christian family and well-adjusted kids, a successful career and healthy bank statement, or a meaningful ministry—and these things are taken away or threatened, suffering will reveal the bankruptcy of our misplaced longings. God gently pries our hands even from the fruit of our lives, so that we can be sustained by abiding in the Vine alone: Jesus, our One and Only.

This, too—this careful separation from the things on which we depend for happiness—takes time. Thankfully, God graciously deals with us, patiently drawing us from our horizontal attachments and implanting within us a desire to attach ourselves fully to himself. It's slow and often painful but it is *purposeful*. There's a point to all of it: "Therefore we do not lose heart. Though outwardly we are wasting away, yet inwardly we are being renewed day by day. For our light and momentary troubles are achieving for us an eternal glory that far outweighs them all. So we fix our eyes not on what is seen, but on what is unseen, since what is seen is temporary, but what is unseen is eternal" (2 Cor. 4:16–18).

In the middle of pruning, life may look like it's falling apart. But on the inside, God is at work, making things new, restoring what's been lost, unfolding his grace in ways we can't understand because we're bound by human limits. Pruning won't last forever, but God promises that the fruit he produces will. Only for the joy set before us can we endure the process of slow growth. Without the hope of eternity, a destination of complete perfection and fulfillment, fruit taking time to ripen and the pain of pruning would be unbearable.

When suffering weighs on you, pull out the ace in your pocket: gratitude. Thank God for everything you know about eternal life: there will be no pain. Thank you, God. There will be no conflict. Thank you, Jesus. There will be no abuse, no betrayal, no disappointment, no fear, no shame. Thank you, thank you, Lord. Giving thanks to God in the midst of suffering breaks the power of pain. It doesn't make it less real or less hurtful, but it no longer has power over you when you offer thanks to God. This is abiding in Jesus.

Remember what we discovered earlier: you don't have to white-knuckle thanks to God for your current predicament. Terminal illness is not good. Family dysfunction is not good. No suffering is good. We can thank God for the things we know *are* good and *are* to come, however, and this gives us enough breathing room to thank God for the gifts that he allows us to enjoy here on earth as well.

Practicing the Prayer of Abiding

In a similar way, the prayer of abiding breaks the tyranny of immediacy and productivity in our hearts. Abiding in Christ involves withdrawing from outward occupations so that you can form the habit of returning to God and making yourself at home in his peaceful, tender love.

One would think we'd all want this. Who wouldn't choose to be at home in a place of grace, acceptance, and serenity? Turns out, many of us! Our daily lives show that we'd rather keep running on the treadmill of "one more thing" (another project to complete, another meal to make, another load of laundry to wash, dry, fold, and put away) than take time to cultivate the quiet attentiveness to the Spirit of God characteristic of abiding.

Abiding is the ultimate surrender of the will—the choice to be with God, ceasing from activity—so that he might accomplish whatever it is that he desires. Sometimes that will be the imparting of knowledge, other times a sense of his presence and love in a powerful way. On some occasions we will feel nothing, sense nothing, and may fear that we've done something wrong. Abiding is not about producing, however; it's mostly about choosing. Choosing to remain. Deciding to stay. Returning over and over to be at home in Jesus. Like ripening fruit, this takes time.

Henri Nouwen writes,

> There is always so much that still has to be done, so many tasks to finish and jobs to work on that simple presence can easily seem

useless and even a waste of our time. But still, without a conscious desire to "waste" our time, it is hard to hear the blessing[s]. . . . They are there, surrounding us on all sides. But we do have to be present to them and receive them. They don't force themselves on us. They are gentle reminders of that beautiful, strong, but hidden, voice of the one who calls us by name and speaks good things about us.[7]

So, how do I—hoping to encourage you to practice abiding—possibly "teach" you how to do something that is neither quantifiable nor focused on a specific outcome, something that's so completely *not about us*, but purely about God? A tough task, to be sure!

The best advice I can give you is to allow abiding to wake you up. Thomas Keating likened it to becoming aware of the air we breathe. We rarely think of the oxygen that we take, moment by moment, into our lungs. Yet there it is, in us and around us at all times! In the same manner, the presence of God is imminently near, within our very souls by the sealing of the Holy Spirit, and we are *in Christ*. Abiding makes us more and more aware of this reality. The purpose of abiding is to awaken us so that we see reality as it is—immersed in God, permeated with his presence, pointing ever and always to his glory.[8]

Don't expect yourself to be immediately "good at this." Even that kind of thinking will inhibit the abiding peace Jesus longs for you to experience. Start small, perhaps with two to five minutes of quiet waiting on God (Isa. 30:18 or Ps. 27:14 can be great verses to read out loud as you begin). This differs slightly from practicing the prayer of silence because abiding prayer focuses strictly on God for his own sake, not for direction, not for listening, but just to be with him. For abiding prayer, some recommend using only a single word (e.g., the name of Jesus or a word like *love*). I like using *Abba*, God's "daddy" name. This prayer word is used to draw you back into Christ's presence when your mind drifts.

Most likely, this will happen often (especially at first), so be gentle with yourself! Using a prayer word is intended to help you remain at home in Christ, not feel berated.

As God awakens you to himself, you may become aware of other things in your soul, too; this can feel flat-out ugly! At the same moment you're seeking to abide, thoughts you might be ashamed of may swim to the surface. This is normal! Abiding is an opportunity to be at home with Jesus even in your yuck. He will not heal what we refuse to acknowledge, for we cannot repent of our own sin or forgive the hurts done to us without seeing them for what they really are. You may wish to write down things that come up during abiding so that you can process through them with a trusted pastor or counselor later on. Don't become so distracted by these thoughts that they steal the time you've set aside for abiding, however.

Whenever and to wherever your mind drifts, use Jesus's name or a loving prayer word to return and remain in his presence. Jesus doesn't want you just to "do" things for him; he wants your heart because he loves you. He longs to make you whole, to heal you; he desires for you to be emotionally healthy, not just spiritually successful. Abiding makes this possible.

As you practice abiding—which involves sitting quietly and patiently allowing God to teach you how to direct your thoughts more and more toward him (and thus away from the things of the earth)—you will notice that you *are* becoming progressively more at home in his presence. Any negative emotions that you feel—the anger that may arise because someone wounded you, the bitterness of a hurt long past, the fear of an uncertainty looming ahead—eventually become fuel for the consuming fire of his presence.

Allow your emotions to be there, to be real; allow yourself to feel them so that Jesus can heal, redeem, and restore you. Remaining in him allows you to be fully you and fully awake to God. It's so real, so raw, and so refreshing. No hiding, no pretending, just being awake to God's sovereign grace over the good, the bad, the ugly, and the glorious unfolding.

There are some excellent guides to contemplative abiding available. I like Adele Calhoun's *Spiritual Disciplines Handbook: Practices That Transform Us*. With a guide like this, you can experiment with various forms of prayerful contemplation to find one or more that resonate with your temperament. Thank God we don't all have to "do" abiding alike. My husband and I spend time with God differently because he made us uniquely and relates to us individually. The same is true for you.

The key is first to choose. Without a deliberate decision to practice abiding, it will not happen. The natural pull of our lives is *away* from Christ (because we live in a sinful, broken world). Without resolve, we drift. Make a choice today to try waiting on God. What do you have to lose? Can you spare two minutes of your time to begin today? Ask him to awaken you to his presence within and around you, even if it's difficult at first. Ask him to help you find a word that brings you gently into his presence. Abiding is actually a foretaste of heaven, where being in his presence will be the most natural and fulfilling part of our existence. Sweet friend, it's worth your wait.

~~~~~

Questions for Personal Reflection or Group Discussion:

1. How have you experienced abiding in the past? What new dimension would you like to explore after reading this chapter?

2. How can focusing on "the joy set before you" help when trials and troubles come?

3. What prayer word do you think could help you gently abide in Jesus?

Recommended Reading:

- Calhoun, Adele. *Spiritual Disciplines Handbook: Practices That Transform Us*, revised and expanded edition. Downers Grove, IL: InterVarsity Press, 2015.
- Scazzero, Peter. *Emotionally Healthy Spirituality: It's Impossible to Be Spiritually Mature, While Remaining Emotionally Immature*. Nashville: Zondervan, 2006.

Benediction

Where do you go from here? What do you do with the knowledge that you are destined for eternal glory, chosen to experience life to the limit, fully known even in the yuck of your life, and set free from the emptiness, shame, fear, and tyranny of productivity? Do you go on your merry way with a "Thanks, Jesus" nod to the Lord?

It seems ridiculously flippant even to write that.

Ultimately, your identity is not purely about you. Your life is all at once too magnificent and your potential too precious to squander on yourself alone. God gives us security so that we can enjoy life beyond our own plans and passions. Every piece of you fits together into a gorgeous design, not only for your life, but also in his plan for the whole world. There's no part of you he leaves out or ignores; nothing is wasted! Knowing our identity in the Great I AM should expand our hearts and vision, not constrict them.

A beautiful picture of this occurred to me as I studied shepherds in the ancient Middle East (never thought I'd be writing that sentence!). These brave men often had no assistance. They employed neither undershepherds nor sheepdogs; they had no technological means to round up their flocks. Instead, they raised bellwether sheep. These chosen lambs were treated as tenderly as family, reared in intimate closeness to the shepherd and guarded as his very own. The shepherd eventually released one or more mature bellwethers to go out into the pasture and bring any stragglers back. The bellwether sheep knew how good it was to be near to the master, and they were trained to bring their fellow sheep back so they could experience his goodness too.

The spiritual parallel is not difficult to draw. As you grow closer to Jesus, you are simultaneously kept near *and* sent out, just like a bellwether. You are nurtured and nourished by the Shepherd himself; your intimate closeness is the sustenance you need. You then go out and do his bidding, returning to him to be filled and cared for once again. Bellwether sheep don't stay out perpetually, nor are they ultimately responsible for the other sheep. That is the shepherd's job, and he wants his treasured ones to be safe, well-fed, and near to him, not just do things for him. He trusts the bellwethers to return because they know where life is found.

Too many Christians think they need to be "out" at all times, busily working for God. They forget that being near to Jesus is the *only* thing they are required to choose. Everything else—all that we are or do "on the outside"—is up to and about him.

As I close this book, I'd like to pray a benediction over you: may you stay so close to the Good Shepherd that you know when it's his will that you go out.

If you do, you can venture into this world with complete confidence and freedom, under his authority and with his clear direction. You go without the burden of having to do or figure everything out. It's not all up to you.

At the same time, you get to participate in his glorious work! Like a bellwether, you get to bring in the hurting and lost, helping them find the way, reminding them of the truth, showing them what it's like to live a resurrected life. What joy this brings!

Webster defines *bellwether* broadly as "someone or something that leads others or shows what will happen in the future."[1] Couldn't have said it better myself! You, as one of God's chosen ones, a daughter who knows her belovedness, her honor in his kingdom, and the satisfaction of being near to him, can now lead others and show them what will happen: the unfolding of God's glory today and throughout eternity.

Revel in it, my beloved sister. I am and will be for all eternity!

Acknowledgments

Abba, Jesus, Spirit of God, thank you. Be exalted in these words and do your kingdom work through them. I am so grateful that you called me out of darkness and into your marvelous light.

Jocelyn Alexandra, you are a fabulous, fiery, and flat-out fun girl! God did such a phenomenal job making you, my sweet Love Bug. I love you *"Until the very end."*

To **Jasmine Alyssa,** my precious Friendbeak: You bring red sunshine into my life every day, and I thank God that he made me your Mama. Don't forget Robin!

Mom and Dad, you have supported me in every possible way. You give feedback, read drafts, discuss endlessly, and continue to shape my adult life in godly ways. Thank you for being the kind of parents I love spending time with. You also rock at being Mimi and Babbo!

To **Kathy Moratto,** your influence has shaped me more than you can possibly know. I think you are absolutely wonderful and know that God does too!

Megan Donovan, you are a tenacious and faithful sister in Christ. I love spending time together and watching God work in and use you for his glory.

To **Jenn Paul,** in whom the Living Water runs deep: I count it a privilege to share life with you, my beloved friend.

Cameron Germann, through the years your fellowship has uplifted and refined me again and again. I am so grateful to know and be known by you.

To **Michelle Ballou,** my precious sister, who serves God with passion and challenges me to do the same: Snoopy forever!

Lynette Fuson, your friendship is a gift from God. I love that we can have deep conversations and crazy fun at the beach on the same day. You are a treasure!

To **Betsy Yphantides,** for so many years and so many amazing memories (perhaps not including 2:00 a.m. wake-up calls at Newport!). I am grateful to God for you in my life.

The ladies of Emmanuel Faith Community Church, especially **Jill Becker, Andrea Douglas, Lynn Burns,** and **Abby Fishbeck,** thank you for encouraging me in the initial stages of developing this book. Your feedback at the Forest Home women's retreat spurred me on to research and write. I am grateful to and for each of you.

To **Rindi Hawkins, Kiri Tavernari, Lizzy Redford, and Tracey Redford,** who graciously read drafts of the proposal and offered insightful feedback. I'm grateful for and love each of you remarkable women!

Louise Moesta, dearest Oma, I cherish you. Though our time in Colorado was short, your impact in my life has been tremendous.

To **Penny Anderson,** one of the most devoted friends and servants of the Lord anywhere! Love you, AP!

Rebekah Guzman, you are an editorial force to be reckoned with! Thank you for sharing many years and many words with me. I praise God for you and love you to pieces!

To **the entire Baker Books team,** including my thorough, thoughtful, and helpful project editor, Laura Peterson—unbiridled thanks!

To **Spencer and Rona Clark,** with tremendous gratitude for your love and encouragement. I am so grateful for your prayers and the way you care for our whole family!

Jeramy Alan, it will always be me and you, JTF! I am blessed to partner with you for the sake of the gospel, the building of God's church, and the growth of our family. I love you more each day, mi amigo.

Notes

Introduction

1. Thoughts in this paragraph were inspired by the work of Pastor Paul David Tripp, whose devotional book, *New Morning Mercies* (Wheaton: Crossway, 2014), impacted me deeply. See devotionals between September 6 and September 11.

Chapter 1 Since You Are Precious and Honored . . .

1. See Leon Festinger, *A Theory of Cognitive Dissonance* (Palo Alto, CA: Stanford University Press, 1957), 3–31.

2. Judith Hougen, *Transformed into Fire: Discovering Your True Identity as God's Beloved* (Grand Rapids: Kregel Publications, 2002), 24.

3. Rose Marie Miller, *From Fear to Freedom* (Colorado Springs: Shaw Books, 1994), 115.

Chapter 2 Do You Want to Be Well?

1. Timothy Keller, *Counterfeit Gods: The Empty Promises of Money, Sex, and Power, and the Only Hope that Matters* (New York: Dutton, 2009), xiv.

2. Kyle Idleman, *Gods at War: Defeating the Idols that Battle for Your Heart* (Grand Rapids: Zondervan, 2013), 213.

3. Keller, *Counterfeit Gods*, 64–65.

4. Ibid.

5. Idleman, *Gods at War*, 60.

6. I've adapted these from Idleman's and Keller's books, which were so foundational in my own idol analysis.

7. C. S. Lewis, *The Voyage of the Dawn Treader* (New York: HarperTrophy, 1994), 106–9.

8. See Thomas Chalmers, *Sermons: Select Works* (Edinburgh: Thomas Constable and Co., 1855), 3:249. Portions are available free online at http://www.ole

missxa.org/wp-content/uploads/2014/06/Expulsive-Power-of-a-New-Affection .pdf, accessed May 23, 2016.

Chapter 3 From Fear to Freedom

1. Marcus Dods, *The Expositor's Bible: The Gospel of St. John, vol. 1*, Kindle edition, locations 4056–63.

2. Henri Nouwen, *Life of the Beloved: Spiritual Living in a Secular World* (New York: Crossroad Publishing Company, 2002), 137.

3. I first came across this idea while reading Tripp, *New Morning Mercies*, January 18, June 30, and August 18,

4. Lewis Smedes, *Shame and Grace: Healing the Shame We Don't Deserve* (New York: HarperCollins, 1993), 5.

5. Brené Brown, *The Gifts of Imperfection: Let Go of Who You Think You're Supposed to Be and Embrace Who You Are* (Center City, MN: Hazelden Publishing, 2010), Kindle edition, 40–41.

6. Ibid., 9–10.

7. Ibid., 11.

8. Linda Hartling, et al., "Shame and Humiliation: From Isolation to Relational Transformation," *Work in Progress* 88 (2000), accessed January 18, 2016 at http:// www.humiliationstudies.org/documents/hartling/HartlingShameHumiliation.pdf.

9. Cheryl Broderson, *When a Woman Lets Go of Her Fears* (Eugene, OR: Harvest House, 2010), 27.

10. Arthur W. Pink, *The Gospel of John* (Prisbrary Publishing, 2012), Kindle edition, locations 10166–10170, emphasis added.

11. Broderson, *When a Woman Lets Go*, 91.

12. Jeanne Guyon, *Experiencing the Depths of Jesus Christ* (Jacksonville: SeedSowers Publishing, 1975), 85.

13. Dr. Caroline Leaf, *Who Switched Off My Brain: Controlling Toxic Thoughts and Emotions* (Southlake, TX: Switch on Your Brain, Ltd., 2007), 49–50.

14. In his book *What Happy People Know*, Dr. Dan Baker writes, "During active appreciation, the threatening messages from your amygdala (fear center of the brain) and the anxious instincts of your brainstem are cut off, suddenly and surely, from access to your brain's neocortex, where they can fester, replicate themselves, and turn your stream of thoughts into a cold river of dread. It is a fact of neurology that the brain cannot be in a state of appreciation and a state of fear at the same time. The two states may alternate, but are mutually exclusive." Dan Baker, PhD, and Cameron Stauth, *What Happy People Know: How the New Science of Happiness Can Change Your Life for the Better* (New York: St. Martin's Press, 2003), 81.

Chapter 4 You're Always In

1. In John chapter 10, the word translated "door" in the NASB and ESV is rendered "gate" by the NIV and NLT. Because my study revealed no significant difference between these terms, they will be used interchangeably throughout the chapter.

2. Pink, *Gospel of John*, locations 8786–8789.

3. Philip Keller, *The Shepherd Trilogy* (Grand Rapids: Zondervan, 1996), 208, 210.

4. C. S. Lewis, "The Inner Ring" (lecture, King's College, University of London, 1944), accessed January 27, 2016 at http://www.lewissociety.org/innerring.php.

5. Ibid.

6. C. H. Spurgeon, "I Am the Door," quoted in ed. Charles Cook, *C.H. Spurgeon's Sermons on Christ's Names and Titles: The Kelvedon Edition* (London: Marshall, Morgan, and Scott, 1961), 113.

7. You can find more in my books *Every Thought Captive: Battling the Toxic Beliefs that Separate Us from the Life We Crave*; *When I Get Married: Surrendering the Fantasy, Embracing the Reality*; and *The Life You Crave: The Promise of Discernment*, available digitally and in print at www.jandjclark.com.

8. For Smedes's thoughts on redemptive remembering and other ideas that shaped my understanding of forgiveness, see Lewis Smedes, *Forgive and Forget: Healing the Hurts We Don't Deserve* (New York: HarperSanFrancisco, 1997), 139 and following.

9. G. K. Chesterton, *The Crimes of England* (A Word to the Wise, 2013), Kindle edition, front matter.

10. Keller, *Shepherd Trilogy*, 119–20.

11. Beth Moore, *Get Out of That Pit: Straight Talk about God's Deliverance* (Nashville: Integrity, 2007), 51–52.

12. Watson wrote under the pseudonym, Ian MacLaren. "Letters: Urges Kindness," signed Ian MacLaren, *Trenton Evening Times*, Trenton, NJ, January 3, 1957.

Chapter 5 Satisfying Your True Hunger

1. John 6:34 NLT 1996.

2. Adaptation of John 6:33–35, 48–51, inspired by Paul Langham, *The Jesus Book: A Fresh Retelling of John's Gospel* (Bath, UK: Creative Publishing, 2008), 17.

3. I like Gregg Matte's treatment of this subject in his book, *I AM Changes Who I Am: Who Jesus Is Changes Who I Am, What Jesus Does Changes What I Am to Do* (Grand Rapids: Baker Books, 2012), 29 and following.

4. Iain Campbell, *I Am: Exploring the "I Am" Sayings of John's Gospel* (Evangelical Press, 2016), Kindle edition, locations 114–16.

5. Shaun Dreisbach, "Shocking Body-Image News: 97% of Women Will Be Cruel to Their Bodies Today," *Glamour*, accessed February 2, 2016 at http://www.glamour.com/health-fitness/2011/02/shocking-body-image-news-97-percent-of-women-will-be-cruel-to-their-bodies-today.

6. Stephanie Pappas, "Many Women Would Trade 1 Year of Life to Be Thin," *Livescience.com*, April 5, 2011, accessed February 2, 2016 at http://www.livescience.com/13574-women-trade-life-thin.html.

7. Dallas Willard, *Renovation of the Heart: Putting on the Character of Christ* (Colorado Springs: NavPress, 2002), 159.

8. Naomi Wolf, *The Beauty Myth: How Images of Beauty Are Used Against Women* (New York: William Morrow, 1991), 52, emphasis added.

9. "The Order for Holy Communion," from *The Book of Common Prayer* (New York: Church Publishing, 1979).

10. Tripp, *New Morning Mercies*, September 29.

11. Andrew Seve, quoted in Hougen, *Transformed into Fire*, 127.

12. Carolyn Costin, *The Eating Disorders Sourcebook: A Comprehensive Guide to the Causes, Treatments, and Prevention of Eating Disorders* (Los Angeles: Lowell House, 1999), 53.

13. As told in Charles Allen, *God's Psychiatry: Healing for Your Troubled Heart* (Grand Rapids: Revell, 2015), 10.

Chapter 6 I'm Not Afraid of the Dark Anymore

1. C. S. Lewis, "They Asked For A Paper," in *Is Theology Poetry?* (London: Geoffrey Bless, 1962), 164–65, accessed February 10, 2016 at http://www.cslewisinstitute.org/Christianity_Makes_Sense_of_the_World.

2. François Fénelon, *Talking with God*, trans. Hal M. Helms (Brewster, MA: Paraclete Press, 1997), 74, 76, and 75.

3. Tripp, *New Morning Mercies*, December 11.

4. Cheryl Brodersen's thoughts on this in *When a Woman Lets Go of the Lies* (Harvest House Publishers, 2012), Kindle edition, 19 were helpful to me in thinking through this issue.

5. Andrew Murray, "The Prayer Life" in *Andrew Murray on Prayer* (New Kensington, PA: Whitaker House, 1998), 186.

6. Mark Buchanan, *The Rest of God: Restoring Your Soul by Restoring Sabbath* (Nashville: Thomas Nelson, 2006), 121.

7. Jamin Goggin and Kyle Strobel, *Beloved Dust: Drawing Close to God by Discovering the Truth About Yourself* (Nashville: Nelson Books, 2014), 41 and 53.

Chapter 7 The Unforced Rhythms of Grace

1. Buchanan, *The Rest of God*, 90, emphasis added.

2. Dr. Timothy Keller, "He Welcomes Sinners" (sermon on Luke 15:1–10, September 28, 2008) available for purchase online at http://www.gospelinlife.com/he-welcomes-sinners-5613.

3. Keller, *Shepherd Trilogy*, 362–63.

4. Keller, "He Welcomes Sinners" sermon.

5. Warren Wiersbe, *Jesus in the Present Tense: The I AM Statements of Christ* (Colorado Springs, CO: David C. Cook, 2011), 81–82.

6. Keller, *Shepherd Trilogy*, 92.

7. Keller, *Shepherd Trilogy*, 97–98.

8. As told in Matte, *I AM Changes Who I Am*, 153.

9. Thanks to Hougen, *Transformed into Fire*, 19 for this image.

10. Buchanan, *The Rest of God*, 45.

11. Lynne Twist, *The Soul of Money: Transforming Your Relationship with Money and Life* (New York: W.W. Norton, 2003), 42.

12. Keller, *Shepherd Trilogy*, 29.

13. Oswald Chambers, "June 14—Get Moving! (1)" in *My Utmost for His Highest*, accessed February 18, 2016, available in modern language at http://utmost.org/get-moving-1/.

14. Oswald Chambers, "Day 10" in *Hope: A Holy Promise* Reading Plan, accessed February 18, 2016, https://www.bible.com/reading-plans/990-oswald-chambers-hope-a-holy-promise/day/10, italics mine.

15. Goggin and Strobel, *Beloved Dust*, 9.

Selah: Introducing the Way, the Truth, and the Life

1. Guyon, *Experiencing the Depths*, 41.

2. Thomas à Kempis, *The Imitation of Christ*, ed. and trans. by Jospeh N. Tylenda (New York: Vintage Spiritual Classics edition, 1998), 167.

Chapter 8 Making Good Decisions in a Choice-Crazy World

1. The fruit of this research became a book titled *The Life You Crave: The Promise of Discernment*, originally published in 2008 by NavPress, now available through Be Transformed Ministries at www.jandjclark.com.

2. Leaf, *Who Switched Off My Brain*, 72.

3. Ibid., 71.

4. See Buchanan, *The Rest of God*, 190–91.

5. Ibid.

6. Mary Geegth, *God Guides* (Zeeland, MI: Mission Partners India, 1995), 7.

7. St. Thomas Aquinas, *Commentary of The Gospel of St. John* (Kindle edition, 2010), locations 12663–12666. Aquinas quotes Augustine here and adds his own thoughts.

8. Warren Wiersbe's thoughts on this in *Jesus in the Present Tense*, Kindle edition, 94, were helpful to me in forming these thoughts.

Chapter 9 Discovering (and Loving!) the Real You

1. C. S. Lewis, *Mere Christianity* in *The Complete C. S. Lewis Signature Classics* (New York: HarperOne, 2002), 176–77.

2. Cicero, *De Amicitia*, chapter 26, Latin text available at http://www.thelatinlibrary.com/cicero/amic.shtml, English translations accessed March 29, 2016 at http://ncpedia.org/symbols/motto.

3. Keller, *Shepherd Trilogy*, 248–49.

4. Scott Underwood, "Take My Life," *Winds of Worship 6*, Vineyard Music, 1996, CD.

5. See Jerusha Clark, *Living Beyond Postpartum Depression: Hope and Help for the Hurting Mom and Those Around Her* (Colorado Springs: NavPress, 2010), available now in digital and print from Be Transformed Ministries at www.jandjclark.com

6. Brennan Manning, *Abba's Child: The Cry of the Heart for Intimate Belonging* (Colorado Springs: NavPress, 2015), 55. Manning quotes his friend Barbara Fiand here.

7. I'm indebted to Judith Hougen for her thoughts on this, which shaped my understanding of authenticity and brokenness. See Hougen, *Transformed into Fire*, 135.

8. Murray, "The Prayer Life," 128 and 130, emphasis added.

9. And also an author whose work I highly recommend! Dr. Lisa Bode's book with Gary Richmond, *Ounce of Protection: Divorce-Proofing Your Marriage* (Ann Arbor, MI: Servant Publications, 1995), is an especially outstanding resource.

10. Joseph Luft and Harry Ingham, "The Johari Window: A Graphic Model of Interpersonal Awareness," *Proceedings of the Western Training Laboratory in Group Development* (Los Angeles: University of California, Los Angeles Press, 1955), accessed October 12, 2016 at http://www.convivendo.net/wp-content/up loads/2009/05/johari-window-articolo-originale1.pdf.

11. Moore, *Get Out of That Pit*, 103.

12. Brown, *Gifts of Imperfection*, 6.

13. Goggin and Strobel, *Beloved Dust*, 155.

14. Guyon, *Experiencing the Depths*, 101 and 109.

Chapter 10 Giving Your Life So That Others Might Live

1. Even one who undergoes gender transformation will always be a woman who was changed, someone who became something other.

2. The author of *Five Aspects of Woman* and a curriculum writer for the International Council for Gender Studies, Barbara Mouser, helped me understand this verse. Her lecture on redeemed life-giving is available free online and I highly recommend it: http://www.5aspects.org/audio/2014audio/5AW_Lesson_12_LGR .mp3, accessed April 21, 2016.

3. Peter Kreeft's excellent essay "Is There Sex in Heaven?" was a particular help for this section. It was originally included in his book, *Everything You Ever Wanted to Know About Heaven* (San Francisco: Ignatius Press, 1990), but you can find the essay online at http://www.peterkreeft.com/topics/sex-in-heaven .htm. Accessed April 22, 2016.

4. Brown, *Gifts of Imperfection*, 66.

5. I appreciate the way Philip Keller describes this in "A Shepherd Looks at the Lamb of God," in *Shepherd Trilogy*, 288–89.

6. Jan Karon, *Out to Canaan* (New York: Penguin, 1997), 337.

Chapter 11 So Much More to Life than This

1. As told by Dr. Howard Hendricks in his message to the International Congress on Biblical Inerrancy in San Diego, March 4, 1982, quoted in R. Kent Hughes, *Acts: The Church Afire* (Wheaton: Crossway Books, 1996), 272.

2. The first seventeen verses of John 15.

3. I highly recommend Jamin Goggin and Kyle Strobel's thoughts on this theme, found in their book, *Beloved Dust*, 119–124.

4. Pink, *Gospel of John*, locations 13545–49.

5. C. S. Lewis, *Mere Christianity* (New York: HarperCollins, 2015), 205, emphasis added.

6. For biblical support of these ideas, see verses like 1 Corinthians 6:19–20, Romans 8:17–18, and 2 Corinthians 3:18, which speak of our position as the Holy Spirit's dwelling place, as well as the glory and suffering we will share with Christ.

7. Nouwen, *Life of the Beloved*, 80–81.

8. Thomas Keating, *Open Mind, Open Heart: The Contemplative Dimension of the Gospel* (New York: Continuum, 2002), 44–45.

Benediction

1. *Merriam-Webster Online*, s.v. "bellwether," accessed May 2, 2016 at http://www.merriam-webster.com/dictionary/bellwether.

Jerusha Clark is the author or coauthor of a dozen books including *Every Thought Captive*, *When I Get Married*, *Living Beyond Postpartum Depression*, and *Your Teenager Is Not Crazy*. Jerusha and her husband, Jeramy, a pastor at Emmanuel Faith Community Church, have two fabulous teenage daughters and enjoy spending as much time as possible at the beach. Jerusha's ministry passion is to help people more fully glorify and enjoy their God.

To learn more about Jerusha's writing
and ministry, visit **jandjclark.com**.

Also Available from
JERUSHA CLARK

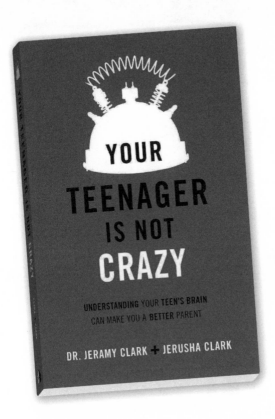

The teenage years. These three words can incite panic in many of us. Will our sweet boy or girl morph into an incomprehensible bundle of hormones and angst? To move from panic to peace, however, we need a change of perspective. Rather than seeing the teen years as a time to simply hold on for dear life, Dr. Jeramy and Jerusha Clark show that adolescence can be an amazing season of cultivating creativity, self-awareness, and passion for the things that really matter.